BUILDING
WEALTH
WHILE
SERVING

A SOLDIER'S GUIDE TO FINANCIAL SUCCESS

GRAMMAR
FACTORY
— ESTᴰ 2013 —

Praise for *Building Wealth While Serving*

"*Building Wealth While Serving* is a refreshing take on personal finance and wealth-building strategies, designed for the soldier, sailor, aviator, or special operator of the Canadian Armed Forces. The author skillfully combines relatable anecdotes with actionable advice, making complex financial concepts accessible and engaging for any military reader. Whether you are a beginner or someone looking to refine your wealth-building strategies, this book is sure to provide valuable insights and motivation on your journey to financial freedom while serving."

ANTHONY JONES, MMM, CD, CWO (Ret'd)

"Wow, this book is destined to become an important guide not just in the Canadian Armed Forces (CAF) world, but in our society. *Building Wealth While Serving* should be a mandatory read for all units to educate and support the well-being of all soldiers and their families. I wish I had read this book 25 years ago when I started serving. It's never too late to start saving and investing—this is the book you need to read."

RAPHAËL DRAPEAU, Sgt (Ret'd)

"After devouring this book cover to cover in less than a weekend, I could not get enough of Paulo's lived financial experiences, shared stories in the ranks, and his focused instructions for wealth and wisdom while serving in the Canadian Armed Forces (CAF). In *Building Wealth While Serving*, Paulo speaks 'soldier' to inform anyone in any rank how possible it is to make your money work for you—not the other way around. From his many examples, he explains how 'operational readiness' applies to everything, including your bank account. So lace up your boots, throw on your ruck, and get ready to follow Paulo Keomanyla's wisdom to turn your pay into your legacy!"

JO PELLERIN, Military spouse

"Coming up through the ranks in the military, members are trained to problem solve, plan, and execute missions given to them from the simplest of tasks to the more complex. All these skills we learn are laid out in an easy-to-follow flow, ensuring operational success. Yet when it comes to personal finances, at times we are all too quick to let common sense go to the wind, to overcomplicate saving for our future, or let the shiny purchases get the better of us. This book is your guide to tackling your personal finances like a mission plan for financial freedom. Now, thanks to *Building Wealth While Serving*, we have the Course of Actions (COAs) to help guide us down the previously uncharted path of wealth building toward personal mission success."

QUINN STEVENSON, CD, WO (Ret'd)

"As a military wife, I've seen firsthand how challenging it can be to manage finances while juggling the unique demands of military life. *Building Wealth While Serving* was such a refreshing and empowering read. Paulo Keomanyla writes with heart, warmth, and a deep understanding of what our community goes through. This isn't just another finance book—it's a practical, down-to-earth guide filled with wisdom that truly speaks to military families. It gave me the confidence to talk more openly about money, make better financial choices, and feel hopeful about the future. I wish we had this book years ago!"

TARA

"*Building Wealth While Serving* is a reminder that we can and *should* always be doing more with our money. Paulo Keomanyla breaks down the invisible barriers that military members place on themselves when it comes to building wealth and offers simple solutions in plain language to overcome those barriers. The After Action Reports at the conclusion of each chapter provide a concise summary of what was covered and act as an excellent personal finance checklist. As a direct result of reading this book, I've made changes to how I go about saving for the future, and I feel confident about those changes. I very much recommend this book to all CAF members, from Aviators to Colonels and beyond—there is motivation and advice in his book for all ranks who want to build wealth today and into retirement."

JENNIFER W.

"*Building Wealth While Serving* is extremely well written and perfectly tailored to our military community. After reading this book, I feel I have more knowledge on different investment opportunities, which will help me make informed investing decisions. I don't feel as scared when I think of terms like stocks or bonds. I wish my husband had read this book when he joined 25 years ago. Knowledge is power."

NATASHA SMITH, Military spouse

"This book should be issued alongside the uniform in basic training! If I had read it at the start of my military career, my financial situation would be in a very different place today. This book doesn't just teach you about money; it transforms how you think about it. In my opinion, this is essential reading for every Canadian Armed Forces (CAF) member, no matter where they are in their career, as it offers the potential to help navigate any financial hurdle that comes their way within our unique environment."

JONATHAN W.

"I love how down-to-earth and straightforward this book is. The military references made it light and fun, and the charts and examples that show spending, saving, and investing strategies were so nice to see—other books about personal finance often don't show any real-life examples and can be difficult to understand. Paulo Keomanyla's *Building Wealth While Serving* has inspired me with its realness and mission for good—I think the world needs more of that."

SHINEA KELLY, Military Spouse

"Finally, sound financial lessons I can put into practice immediately. After reading *Building Wealth While Serving*, I feel inspired to make changes that will set me up for a brighter financial future. However, I am not ready to give up my horse addiction yet! On a more serious note, the retirement section made me realize I need to plan better. Thank you for educating me."

SANDA ALLEN, Teacher and military spouse

BUILDING WEALTH WHILE SERVING

Paulo Keomanyla

Building Wealth While Serving
Copyright © 2025 by Lo Xan Keomanyla.
All rights reserved.

Published by Grammar Factory Publishing, an imprint of MacMillan
Company Limited.

Grammar Factory Publishing
MacMillan Company Limited
25 Telegram Mews, 39th Floor, Suite 3906
Toronto, Ontario, Canada
M5V 3Z1

www.grammarfactory.com

Keomanyla, Paulo
Building Wealth While Serving: A Soldier's Guide to Financial
Success / Paulo Keomanyla.

Paperback ISBN 978-1-998528-39-4
Hardcover ISBN 978-1-998528-41-7
eBook ISBN 978-1-998528-40-0

1. BUS027000 BUSINESS & ECONOMICS / Personal Finance / General.
2. BUS050000 BUSINESS & ECONOMICS / Personal Finance / Money
Management.
3. BUS012000 BUSINESS & ECONOMICS / Personal Finance / Military
Personnel.

Production Credits
Cover design by Designerbility
Interior layout design by Setareh Ashrafologhalai
Book production and editorial services by Grammar Factory Publishing

Grammar Factory's Carbon Neutral Publishing Commitment
Grammar Factory Publishing is proud to be neutralizing the carbon footprint of all printed copies of its authors' books printed by or ordered directly
through Grammar Factory or its affiliated companies through the purchase of
Gold Standard-Certified International Offsets.

Disclaimer
The material in this publication is of the nature of general comment only and
does not represent professional advice. It is not intended to provide specific
guidance for particular circumstances, and it should not be relied on as the
basis for any decision to take action or not take action on any matter which it
covers. Readers should obtain professional advice where appropriate, before
making any such decision. To the maximum extent permitted by law, the
author and publisher disclaim all responsibility and liability to any person,
arising directly or indirectly from any person taking or not taking action
based on the information in this publication.

DISCLAIMER

THIS BOOK IS intended for educational purposes only. It is not, nor should it be construed as, investment, financial, or professional advice. The content provided covers general financial topics relevant to a military audience and is not personalized financial guidance for any individual. You are in command of your financial decisions, and it is your responsibility to seek out qualified professionals if you need tailored advice for your specific situation. This book is the result of my personal journey—over twenty years of service, saving, planning, investing, and pursuing financial independence. It reflects the strategies and principles that have worked for me, as well as lessons learned from other experiences that shaped my perspective on building and managing wealth. However, this is not an all-encompassing guide or a definitive blueprint for success. The anecdotes and case studies in this work stem exclusively from my individual journey and should not be interpreted as reflecting the views or practices of the wider Canadian Armed Forces (CAF). This book is published in a private capacity, and I do not speak as a CAF representative. This book is not endorsed by the CAF or the Department of National Defence.

This guide was crafted to arm you with actionable strategies for mastering your financial future and confronting fiscal challenges with confidence. Consider this book one piece of your financial training program. A resource to help you expand your knowledge and make informed decisions. Just as you rely on a variety of tools and tactics to accomplish a mission, use this book as part of a broader strategy to achieve financial readiness and independence. Your financial success depends on your commitment to learning, adapting, and acting on it. Approach your financial journey with the same focus and preparedness you bring to your military duties.

In the skies he soared with courage, and on the ground, his legacy remains grounded in honour, service, and dedication.

In memory of Dave Domagala, a true hero of the Royal Canadian Air Force, whose spirit will forever fly high.

CONTENTS

PREFACE
MISSION STATEMENT

WHEN I SET out to write this book, my mission was simple—to share the hard-earned lessons I learned while juggling two jobs, a military career, and a university education. Picture this—by day, I was a full-time CAF member, and by night, I was delivering chicken wings to hungry strangers while cramming for exams. It was like being stuck in a never-ending field exercise, except the only debrief was my bank account signalling a red alert. But that chaotic chapter of my life taught me more about money management and economic responsibility than any textbook ever could. My story is one of growth, from modest beginnings to building a six-figure net worth in a relatively short time, with my sights set on hitting seven figures before I hang up my uniform. Back then, as a young CAF member, I dreamed of financial success, and now I want to help you chase that same dream, if financial success is in your line of sight. This book is rooted in real-life experiences, the kind you can't make up, and it's designed to spark constructive conversations about money that truly resonate and make sense in everyday life.

One of my biggest motivations for writing this book is to empower you, the future financial leaders, to become symbols of success. With a little dedication and a lot of focus, you can create meaningful change in your life and the lives of those around you. Think of it as leading a platoon, but instead of navigating a minefield, you're navigating your finances. (Spoiler alert—both require a solid plan and the ability to avoid blowing things up.)

Now, full disclosure—I haven't always been a financial genius. In my younger years, I spent money as if I were auditioning for a TV show titled *Who Can Drain Their Bank Account the Fastest?* I bought things I didn't need, ignored the things I did, and had zero clue about investing. My financial education consisted of "don't spend it all at once," which, let's be honest, is about as useful as a screen door on a submarine. School taught me algebra and how to dissect a frog, but not how to budget, save, or invest. And I'm willing to bet I'm not the only one who felt like they were thrown into the global economy with no map and a broken compass. I've been there too. Early in my career, I thought monetary management was just about paying bills on time and saving whatever was left at the end of the month. It wasn't until I faced a financial setback, a sudden expense that wiped out my bank account, that I realized I needed a better plan. That moment was my wake-up call. I started educating myself, seeking advice, and taking control of my finances. The good news? You don't have to figure it all out on your own. Just as we rely on our training and teamwork to succeed in the military, we can apply those same principles to our finances.

It starts with acknowledging the problem, committing to change, and taking small, consistent steps toward improvement. But here's the thing—I'm not here to lecture you with complex charts or theories that sound like they were invented by someone who owns a monocle. Instead, my goal is to provide you with clear, actionable steps to take control of your finances. Think of it like a set of well-defined protocols. Straightforward, easy to follow, and flexible enough to let you move at your own pace. No confusing jargon or hard-to-decipher acronyms (unlike some military manuals), just practical guidance to help you build momentum. Because let's be real, comparing your financial journey to someone else's is like comparing your push-up count to your Personal Service Program (PSP) trainer who does CrossFit six times a week. It's not helpful, and it's probably going to make you feel bad about yourself.

So, why did I write this book? It all started with a simple question: *"What can I leave behind and how can an average soldier like me offer financial wisdom to those who might be struggling?"* The answer is simple: practical manoeuvres. I'll break it down for you. Avoid overspending, save like your retirement depends on it (because it does), and start investing as soon as you earn a paycheque. Believe it, your future self will thank you. Throughout this book, I'll tackle questions like: How much money do you need to start investing? How can saving for retirement simplify your life? And how do you live frugally without feeling like you're missing out on life? (Hint—it involves fewer eight-dollar lattes and more meal prepping.)

This book is a mix of financial insights and military experiences, and I share both my failures and successes to show you why taking control of your finances matters. It's a call to action, a wake-up call to the financial principles that can transform your present and future. Whether you're just starting out or looking to refine your strategies, this guide is your tactical companion to achieving stability, building wealth, and securing a brighter future for yourself and those who depend on you.

So, grab your rucksack, soldier; we've got some marching to do!

INTRODUCTION

WITH OVER TWENTY YEARS of military experience, I've learned that success, whether on missions or in personal finance, requires discipline, strategy, and adaptability. Throughout my career, I've been deployed on operations that demanded meticulous planning, resilience in the face of uncertainty, and the ability to adapt to rapidly changing conditions. These same principles apply to building wealth. Just as no two missions are the same, no two financial journeys are identical, but the lessons learned in service can guide us toward financial success.

Growing up in an immigrant family, I learned early that building wealth is not just about money. It's about resilience, sacrifice, and the relentless pursuit of opportunity. My parents came to this country with little more than hope and a determination to provide a better future for their children. They worked tirelessly, often in jobs that demanded long hours and offered little pay, but they never quit. Their sacrifices became the foundation of my understanding of what it means to build something from nothing.

For first-generation families like mine, the path to financial stability is often riddled with obstacles. There's no generational wealth to fall back on, no family connections to open doors, and no safety net to cushion the blows of life's uncertainties. Every dollar earned is hard-fought, and every step forward feels like climbing a mountain. My parents taught me the value of frugality and resourcefulness. Lessons that have stayed with me throughout my life and military career. We didn't have the latest gadgets or fancy vacations, but we had enough, and that was a victory in itself.

In the military, I've seen similar struggles among my fellow service members. Many of us come from backgrounds where financial literacy wasn't a priority, and the concept of building wealth feels foreign or out of reach. But just like my parents, we understand the importance of hard work and perseverance. The military provides a certain degree of financial stability, but it's up to us to take that foundation and build upon it. Whether it's through investing in education, starting a side business, or simply learning how to budget effectively to strengthen your financial future, the opportunities are there for those willing to seize them.

One of the most important lessons I've learned is that wealth isn't just about accumulating money; it's about creating opportunities for yourself and others. As soldiers, we have a unique responsibility to look out for one another, both on and off the battlefield. By sharing knowledge, resources, and support, we can help each other break the cycle of financial struggle and build a legacy of prosperity.

My journey has taught me that wealth is not a destination, but a process. It's about making intentional choices, learning from setbacks, and never losing sight of the bigger picture. For those of us who started with nothing, every step forward is a testament to our strength and determination. And as we continue to serve, we have the power to uplift not only ourselves but also those around us, ensuring that the next generation has a stronger foundation than we did.

This book is my way of giving back to the military community that has given me so much. It's a toolkit to help you navigate the financial challenges of military life. From frequent moves to deployments, you can build a secure financial future for yourself and your family. Each chapter of this book will build on your knowledge of personal finance, from basic principles through to how you can invest and assess your wealth as it grows. Together, we can turn the lessons of service into a blueprint for financial success.

CHAPTER 1: MISSION READY

To begin building lasting wealth, start with a strong foundation. This chapter introduces essential financial literacy principles, guides you in setting clear, goal-aligned objectives, and cultivates the mindset needed for sustained success.

CHAPTER 2: STRATEGIC PLANNING

A thriving financial future begins with a strategic plan. This chapter explores proven wealth-building strategies, arming you to craft a blueprint for saving, investing, and growing your assets. With a clear roadmap (the Wheel of Wealth), you'll learn how to make money work effectively for you.

CHAPTER 3: RECONNAISSANCE

Understanding your risk tolerance requires understanding your current financial landscape. This chapter covers various types of investment options and how to assess them. You'll gain the knowledge to make informed decisions about allocating your money across stocks, bonds, real estate, or other opportunities.

CHAPTER 4: TACTICAL EXECUTION

Putting your strategy into action is where wealth building comes to life. This chapter explores asset allocation for effective diversification, guides you in selecting the proper investment accounts, and outlines how to take your first steps, set a timeline, and adjust your plan as needed to stay on track.

CHAPTER 5: BATTLE DRILLS

Financial resilience is crucial for sustained wealth. This chapter offers practical strategies to overcome personal and financial barriers, address financial challenges, and plug money leaks. While protecting your wealth by emphasizing growth, you'll learn about common pitfalls to maintain progress.

CHAPTER 6: SUPPLY LINES

Limited resources require smart money management. This chapter guides you in building a strong support system during service for a smooth transition into life after duty, explores financial challenges you may face post-service, and explains how to prepare for them.

CHAPTER 7: COMMAND AND ALLIANCE

A strong financial plan prospers with a strong team. This chapter equips you to lead your financial team, select the right partners, and maintain clear communication to stay aligned with your goals.

CHAPTER 8: MISSION ACCOMPLISHED

Achieving financial success comes from a well-executed plan. This chapter guides you through evaluating your progress, helps you uncover your own definition of financial success, and celebrates wins. It also covers giving back to your community and ensuring your legacy endures for future generations.

When you become financially literate, you're no longer at the mercy of chance or circumstance. You gain the ability to make informed decisions, create opportunities, and build a life on your own terms. Financial literacy is more than knowledge; it's control over your future.

MISSION READY
UNDERSTANDING FINANCIAL FUNDAMENTALS

ATTENTION! GETTING A grip on financial basics is just as crucial to your personal success as tactical training is to mission readiness. For service members, mastering the essentials—budgeting, saving, investing, and, above all, financial literacy—lays the groundwork for making smart, strategic decisions that affect both your career and your off-duty life. Just as you rely on discipline and focus to accomplish objectives in the field, these same qualities are essential for building a secure financial future. In this first chapter, we'll break down three key elements that will help you take control of your finances:

1 The Terrain: Financial Literacy
2 Mission Plan: Setting Clear Goals
3 Focus and Discipline: The Right Mindset

At the end of this chapter, you'll have the basic tools and understanding to take control of your financial situation, set realistic objectives, and build a secure future with a locked-in mindset. Just as you train to be mission ready on duty, this chapter will help you get financially mission ready so you can tackle your financial objectives with the same focus and determination you bring to your service. *Fall in, soldiers!*

Many of us don't think that managing money is a big deal until it bites us later, or when it's too late. It's often during conversations with peers when we realize that lots of people lack even basic financial knowledge. For most people, understanding and managing money isn't a priority— it's not even on their radar. While a handful actively pursue wealth-building strategies, financial planning remains a mystery to most people.

What's even more troubling is that some of you warriors in the CAF, despite years of service, may not have much to show in terms of savings. It's frustrating, isn't it? CAF members often earn competitive salaries compared to other public sector jobs, yet many still struggle to save when the month ends. How did we end up here? Why aren't we better at managing our finances?

Well, let's face it: We soldiers are good at a few things. For example, we can organize a field exercise in the middle of nowhere, in -40 °C weather, with nothing but a map, a compass, and a questionable Individual Meal Package (IMP) that may or may not be "expired." We can build a bridge out of sticks and hope, or coordinate a multinational operation with allies who, despite all speaking different languages, somehow agree that Tim Hortons is the real Most Valuable Player (MVP). Yet, when it comes to managing our money, we somehow think buying an $89,000 truck on a twelve-year loan is a good idea because "it's got a great sound system." Why is this? Well, let's break it down.

Stand at ease! First, the military is excellent at logistics. We can move an entire battalion across the country, complete with armoured vehicles, tents, and enough coffee to fuel a small nation. But when it comes to moving money from our paycheques into a savings account? Suddenly, it's like we're trying to solve a Rubik's Cube blindfolded. We can plan a deployment down to the last bullet, but budgeting for groceries—that's a bridge too far.

Secondly, we're great at following orders. Tell a soldier to dig a trench, and they'll dig the best darn trench you've ever seen. But tell that same soldier to "stop buying energy drinks at the CANEX store," and suddenly it's mutiny. We'll follow a 300-page operations manual to the letter, but a simple budget spreadsheet is where we draw the line. And let's not forget our love of shiny things. The military spends billions on state-of-the-art equipment because, well, we need to be ready for anything. But when it comes to personal finances, that same mentality kicks in. "Do I need this $389 tactical watch that can survive a nuclear blast?" Probably not. "But what if I'm ever in a nuclear blast?" Better safe than sorry, right?

So, why aren't we better at managing our money? Maybe it's because we're too busy being good at everything else. Or maybe it's because we've been conditioned to believe that "operational readiness" applies to everything except our bank accounts. Either way, it's time to channel some of that military precision into our finances. After all, if we can survive a week in the field with nothing but a tarp, wet wipes, and a dream, we can figure out how to save for retirement. Or at least stop buying so many energy drinks.

Let's be real! Many CAF members could've avoided financial disasters if they'd just been a little more mindful of their spending habits earlier in their careers. At twenty-one years old, pulling in $72,000 as a young Corporal or over $100,000 as a fresh-faced officer feels like winning the lottery. But without the right financial training, it's like handing a private the keys to a G-Wagon and saying, "Good luck, don't crash." Spoiler alert—there's a crash. With a bit of financial guidance, though, many of us could've dodged those money landmines altogether. With a few smart habits formed early on, we might've avoided the financial distress.

But no, we're out here buying brand-new Ford F-150s like we're auditioning for a truck commercial. Unless you're running a moving company or moonlighting as a construction worker, do you really need a truck for your daily commute? Have you ever thought about the fuel costs? And let's not even get started on the other "essentials" we convince ourselves we need, like a personal armoury, a speedboat, two snowmobiles, the latest Jordans, a Ducati and a Harley Davidson (because why choose one?), or even a pet to fill the void of companionship (pro tip—pets are adorable but also financial black holes. Just ask anyone who's ever paid for a dog's emergency surgery).

It's wild that in this age of high-tech everything, where you can learn how to do anything from fixing a carburetor to baking sourdough bread on YouTube, many of us still struggle to save a dime. If you're reading this, though, you've already taken the first step toward turning things around. Whether you're here to strengthen your financial position or just curious about where to start, consider this book your mission brief. If building wealth is your objective, you're in the right place. Let's commit to disciplined financial strategies, prioritize long-term stability over short-term gains, and march toward financial victory. If this resonates with you, consider this book the beginning of your financial career.

Now, let's get to work. We have a mission to complete!

Whether you're managing day-to-day expenses while deployed or mapping out big financial moves for life after the military, a solid grasp of financial principles is your best tool for making smart, informed decisions that fit your unique lifestyle and goals. Now, you might be wondering, how does one build wealth?

1   **Inheritance**—a fortunate few may receive wealth passed down through their family, but this isn't a realistic option for most of us. Not everyone starts with a financial head start, and that's okay.

2   **Theft**—sure, some might entertain the idea of taking shortcuts, but let's be honest: this path is not only unethical but also comes with serious consequences. It's a no-go for anyone committed to integrity and long-term stability.

3   **Hard work**—putting in the effort is essential, but hard work alone doesn't always translate into financial success. It's an important piece, but not the entire puzzle.

4   **Winning the lottery**—while it's possible, it's highly unlikely. The chances of winning are so low that it should never be relied upon as a strategy for building wealth. Statistically, you're more likely to be struck by lightning than win the jackpot. Relying on luck is not a strategy. It's a gamble.

In my experience, the roadmap to building wealth boils down to this: *SAVE, INVEST*, and *REPEAT*. It's a straightforward cycle, but it's incredibly powerful when you stick to it.

Let's cut to the chase: Every CAF member can become wealthy. The CAF pension plan is like the Aircraft Carriers of retirement packages. Reliable, built to last, and something you can count on when the mission is over. If you put in your twenty-five years and retire, you're looking at 50% of your best five years of pay *for life*. That's not just a pension; that's a financial air strike in your favour. If you do the math, with good health and a little luck, your pension could easily add up to nearly or even exceed a cool million dollars over your lifetime. That's right, the moment you raise your hand and swear in, you've got the potential to become a millionaire. It's like having a secret financial weapon in your kit, just waiting to be deployed.

While the CAF pension is a solid foundation, it's not the whole battle plan. Like your base camp, it's essential but not enough to win the war on financial independence. The real mission is to build on that foundation, like investing wisely and making your money work as hard as you do. Because let's face it, if you can push through Physical Training (PT) at 0600 in the middle of February, you've got what it takes to tackle a budget and stick to a solid investment plan. Every CAF member has the potential to do more than just get by financially; you can thrive. The tools are there, and the strategy is clear.

The question is, are you ready to execute the mission?

How you handle your finances during your career has a huge impact on both your wealth and the quality of your retirement. The most important step is simply to start. The sooner you get going, the better the result. We'll dig deeper into this when we tackle retirement planning and its specific challenges, but for now, just remember—every mission begins with that first daring step.

For years, I pondered the question: "How can I build wealth on a CAF salary?" For a time, I accepted my bi-monthly paycheque and didn't think much of it. But as I grew older, I became increasingly concerned about my future financial stability. I started focusing on my retirement and future lifestyle, and soon realized I needed to act. I dug into the numbers to understand my current situation and began planning for my future. That's when I realized the importance of change. I was halfway through my career, yet not on track to achieve the financial goals I had set for myself.

Building wealth or becoming a millionaire is no easy feat. It demands relentless perseverance, tactical patience, and the discipline to overcome every obstacle in your path. True wealth is built, not given. With a strategic approach and disciplined financial habits, you can greatly increase your chances of achieving financial independence and start building the kind of wealth that secures a future that lasts.

THE TERRAIN: FINANCIAL LITERACY

Building wealth goes far beyond simply depositing your salary or relying on your CAF pension after your service. It demands a proactive approach and strategic execution. You've got to learn how to navigate the financial landscape on your own. Just as mastering the skills of a gunner, meteorological technician, or pilot is vital to being ready for any mission, financial literacy is essential for getting your personal finances on the right path. Financial literacy is the bedrock of wealth building. It's the knowledge and skills you need to make informed decisions about your money. Without it, you're like a soldier heading into battle without a map or a weapon. Completely unprepared.

What is Financial Literacy?

Financial literacy means understanding how money works and using that knowledge to handle your personal finances effectively. It's about mastering budgeting, saving, investing, and planning for the future. For many service members, financial literacy is like the missing firing pin in a rifle. Without it, the whole system doesn't function. You might excel at your job, but if you are missing one key component to manage your money, you're setting yourself up for avoidable stress and challenges.

Think of it this way, in the military, you wouldn't send a soldier into the field without proper training. Yet, when it comes to finances, many of us are sent into the world with little to no preparation. We're expected to figure it out as we go, which often leads to costly mistakes. The military life isn't exactly a predictable 9-to-5 gig. Between frequent postings, deployments, and the occasional bombshell, financial planning can feel like trying to assemble your weapon without instructions. It's frustrating and prone to fail. That's why financial literacy isn't just a nice-to-have—it's a must-have for every CAF member.

Take postings, for example. Getting posted to a new Canadian Forces Base (CFB) is like being handed a mission with no intel. Without a budget or an emergency fund, you might find yourself scrambling to cover moving costs, setting up a new place, or handling unexpected expenses like a broken-down car or a surprise bill. But if you've got financial literacy in your toolkit? You're prepared. You've got a plan, a stash of cash for emergencies, and the confidence to confront the high seas ahead.

How To Build Financial Literacy

Building financial literacy doesn't require a finance degree or hours of complicated study. It's about learning the basics and applying them consistently. Here are a few steps to get you started:

1   **Educate Yourself**—read books, take online courses, or attend workshops on personal finance.

2   **Ask Questions**—don't be afraid to seek advice from financially experienced individuals, advisers or mentors.

3   **Practise**—apply what you learn by creating a budget, tracking your spending, and setting financial goals.

Did you know that there are tons of online platforms offering free courses to boost your financial literacy? Take INTUIT, for example—the folks behind the famous Turbo-Tax that many people rely on for filing their taxes. They also offer free basic financial training! You can dive into understanding credit, get a handle on money basics, and explore self-paced courses that help you build the skills to make confident financial decisions. It's like having a financial coach in your kitbag.

It's that simple. By arming yourself with financial knowledge, you're taking the crucial first step toward building wealth and eventually achieving financial independence. Keep in mind the words of Socrates, *"There is only one good, knowledge, and one evil, ignorance."* Ignorance leaves you vulnerable; knowledge is your tactical advantage and will help you make smart choices with your money.

Your Own Terrain Assessment
As you embark on this mission, I challenge you to reflect on the same questions I once asked myself. Questions that reshaped my own financial journey:

- How confident are you in your financial skills?
- Are you currently facing any financial challenges?
- Do you know your net worth?

- Are you satisfied with your financial situation?
- Does money significantly impact your life?
- How do you manage stress related to money?
- Do you aspire to improve your lifestyle?

Your answers will serve as the foundation for your financial plan. Additionally, consider these essential practices:

- Do you maintain a budget to track your spending?
- Is there an emergency fund for unexpected expenses?
- Are you equipped with the right financial support?

Financial Preparedness

At the dawn of my career, I was unprepared financially when I received my first posting message. At the time, I hadn't budgeted for the unexpected costs that come with relocation, such as security deposits, moving supplies, and temporary housing. To make matters worse, I didn't have anyone to rely on for help or advice. I found myself scrambling to cover expenses, dipping into savings I didn't really have, and even relying on credit cards to make ends meet. It was a stressful and humbling experience that left me feeling overwhelmed and frustrated. That relocation taught me a valuable lesson—financial preparedness is non-negotiable. I realized that I needed to take control of my finances, educate myself, and plan for the unforeseen. I started by creating a budget, building an emergency fund, and learning about the resources available to service members during relocations. Over time, I became more confident in managing my money, and I vowed never to be caught off guard again.

Once you get a handle on managing your money, you create space to save and grow it. This shift doesn't just ease stress, it unlocks opportunities, whether that's investing, buying a home, or securing your family's future. Over time, these steps help you build wealth, one step at a time.

Financial literacy is your greatest ally in building and safeguarding your wealth while securing future stability. If certain financial terrain feels unfamiliar, like investments, taxes, or retirement planning, there's no harm in calling in reinforcements. Call in the SMEs (Subject Matter Experts). Financial advisers are like your reconnaissance (RECON) team; they gather critical intel and develop strategies customized to your goals (we'll explore this more later). They'll help you spot blind spots and turn confusion into confidence.

So, arm yourself with knowledge first, and you'll be ready to advance, tackling your financial future with confidence and precision.

MISSION PLAN: SETTING CLEAR GOALS

Your financial mission planning is your big picture objective. The "why" behind every dollar you save, invest, or spend. It's the North Star that guides your financial decisions, whether you're buying a home, ensuring your family's security, or planning for retirement. Just like a military operation, your financial mission should align with your core values and short or long-term vision. To define your mission, start by asking yourself:

- What matters most to me?
- What am I trying to achieve with money?
- What do I want my financial future to look like?
- How can I balance my military commitments with my personal goals?

Defining Your Financial Mission

Your financial mission might sound like this: to build a secure financial future for my family while maintaining a balanced lifestyle that honours my military service. Or, if you're a solo operator, it might be: to achieve financial independence by age forty-five, allowing me to retire comfortably, travel the world, and pursue my passions without financial stress.

Alright, all hands on deck! Your mission statement doesn't need to be fancy; it should just be clear and meaningful to you.

Grab your map, set your coordinates, and put on your gear; your financial mission planning starts now!

Setting Financial Goals, Operational-Style

Once you've defined your mission, break it down into "OPERATIONAL-STYLE" goals. I call it the OPERA—organized, practical, effective, result-driven, and accountable. Here's how to apply the OPERA to your finances:

Say you're a Corporal earning $72,000 a year and your main financial goal is to buy a home. Your OPERA might look something like this: save $25,000 for a down payment within the next two years. Now, let's break it down, OPERA-style:

✓ **Organized**—your goal has a clear structure. You're not just tossing money into a savings account and hoping for the best. You've got a plan, like saving for that down payment. *Check!*

✓ **Practical**—this goal is doable. It's not some far-off, unrealistic idea. It's something you can pull off if you stay disciplined and stick to your budget. *Check!*

✓ **Effective**—your goal has a real purpose. Saving for a home isn't just about acquiring a property; it's about building your future. It's a goal that's going to pay off. *Check!*

✓ **Results-driven**—your goal has a clear finish line. You'll know you've nailed it when you hit that $25,000 mark. No vague moving targets here, just a solid objective. *Check!*

✓ **Accountable**—you've got a timeline (two years) to keep you on track. It's like having a countdown to mission success. You can measure your progress and stay on target. *Check!*

This is how you take a big, daunting goal and break it down into smaller, manageable steps, just like you would with any mission. Instead of feeling overwhelmed, you tackle it piece by piece, turning what seems impossible into something you can execute.

Prioritizing Your Goals

Troops! We know not all missions are created equal. Some are urgent and need immediate attention, while others can be tackled later. The same goes for your financial goals. You can't handle everything all at once. Trying to do so is like showing up to a firefight with no ammo and a busted radio. You need to prioritize. Here's how I break down my financial goals into a tiered system, just like how we rank mission priorities:

Tiers System

Tier 1: Immediate Needs—The "Life or Death" Missions
These are your non-negotiables. The goals that keep you and your family secure, like your financial "combat readiness" checklist.

- Build an emergency fund
- Pay off high-interest debt
- Cover basic living expenses

Tier 2: Medium-Term Goals—The "Strategic Objectives"
Once your immediate needs are covered, shift your focus to goals that will set you up for long-term success. These are your financial force multipliers.

- Save for a down payment on a home
- Invest in your education or career advancement
- Pay off lower-interest debt

Tier 3: Long-Term Aspirations—The "Big Picture" Missions
These are your stretch goals. The ones that require patience, discipline, and a solid plan. This is your financial endgame.

- Save for retirement
- Build generational wealth
- Plan for big-ticket items, like an Aston Martin Vantage. *Hey, to each their own!*

The Rules of Engagement

Focus on Tier 1 goals first. Once those are under control, move on to Tier 2. Tier 3 goals are important, but they're not urgent. Trying to tackle all three tiers at once is like trying to run an operation without ammunition, a recipe for disaster. Remember, prioritizing your goals isn't about giving up on your dreams; it's about executing them in the right order. Successful operation comes from discipline, strategy, and knowing when to advance. This also means monitoring your progress and adjusting your plans.

Just as you would review mission outcomes, regularly assess your financial progress. Set monthly or quarterly check-ins to evaluate whether you're still on track to meet your goals. Life events like deployments or unexpected bills might throw you off course, so stay flexible and be ready to adjust your plan when needed.

Roger that, soldier?

FOCUS AND DISCIPLINE: THE RIGHT MINDSET

Building wealth is like PT, except instead of burpees, you're doing budget burpees, and instead of a six-pack, you're working toward that six-figure bank account. It's not glamorous, and it sure as heck doesn't happen overnight. But just like PT, the more you show up and put in the work, the closer you get to your ideal shape. You don't go to the gym once, do a single push-up, and expect to wake up looking like a bodybuilder. Nope. It takes time, sweat, and a whole lot of discipline. The same goes for your finances. You won't become a millionaire by scrolling through investment tips on Instagram (I've tried). However, by harnessing discipline and consistently putting in effort, you'll see progress over time. Without discipline, even the best-laid plans can fall apart.

Discipline in Action

What is discipline? Discipline is what separates those who achieve their financial goals from those who don't. It's about making consistent, intentional choices with your money, even when it's hard. When it comes to your finances, discipline is just as critical. It's easy to blow your paycheque on a new set of rims for your truck or a spontaneous trip to Vegas. But discipline means sticking to your budget and prioritizing your long-term goals. It's about feeding rounds to your financial magazine (mag), not just your cravings for Tim Hortons iced cappuccinos and tactical gear. And just like you fuel your body with the right nutrients (okay, and maybe the occasional poutine), you need to nourish your financial knowledge. Stay informed, seek out financial news, and look for opportunities to grow your expertise. Managing your finances is like managing your fitness routine. Consistency is key, and skipping leg day will only set you back.

Stay Committed to Your Financial Mission

Staying focused requires regular reminders of why your goals matter. Write it down and keep it somewhere visible, like on your fridge (I put mine on my phone display all the time!). When you're tempted to overspend, remind yourself of the bigger picture. If you're saving for a down payment on a home, every time you're tempted to buy something you don't need, ask yourself: Is this worth delaying my dream of homeownership? Discipline and persistence are your battle buddies on the path to financial realization. Find your *why*; that driving force that keeps you advancing even when the mission gets tough. Shield yourself from distraction, set clear objectives, and take small, consistent steps. If the process feels overwhelming, remember you don't have to go at it alone.

Embracing Accountability

Accountability isn't just a fancy word—it's about being a good soldier. You show up for roll call, you keep your gear squared away, and you answer to your chain of command. The same principle applies to your finances. If you want to stay disciplined and on line up, you need to embrace accountability.

Share your financial goals with someone you trust, like a mentor, your partner, or even a battle buddy who's also on the path to building wealth. Just like you'd rely on a senior

Non-Commissioned Member (NCM) to guide you through a tough mission, a financial adviser can provide expert advice and keep you focused on your objectives. Yes, they'll charge for their services, kind of like that personal trainer who yells at you to do one more chin-up, but their insights can be invaluable. Use them strategically, consult with them as necessary, and leverage their expertise to sharpen your wealth-building strategy. They might just have the tactical tips you need to push you further (more on financial advice provision later).

My biggest financial regret in life is not having sought more advice and not having delved deeper into personal finance earlier. If I'd known two decades ago what I know today, I'd probably be retired at thirty, toes in the sand, coffee in hand. But here's the Operation Order: Regrets are just intel for your next move. Start now! Time's your greatest ally. The sooner you deploy and begin your wealth-building journey, the sooner you'll see results.

The CAF has your six when it comes to money matters. Programs like the Service Income Security Insurance Plan (SISIP) offer tailored financial advice and insurance designed and built from the ground up for the military lifestyle. Your own Quick Reaction Force (QRF) is ready to roll when you need it. Whether you're stressing out over a last-minute posting, trying to figure out retirement without losing your mind, or just wanting to budget for a new vehicle without torching your bank account, SISIP's advisers have got you covered. Their advisers are like your personal overwatch. They've dealt with everything from privates buried under mess bills to Warrants (WO) balancing house payments and kids' tuition. You name it, they've seen it. Call them up, it's like calling in air support before the whole operation goes off the rails.

In today's digital age, building wealth and learning about investing has never been easier. You don't need to be stuck in a classroom or even at home. Deployed overseas? Download a podcast on compound interest during your downtime. Stuck in the mess hall? Pull up a YouTube video like Blueprint Financial on tax perks or Exchange Traded Funds (ETF) investing between bites. Books like *The Wealthy Barber* and *Rich Dad Poor Dad* are your field manuals, breaking down money manoeuvres into Standard Operating Procedures (SOPS). Budgeting apps? That's your financial GPS. Apps like Mint or Wealthsimple don't care if you're in Valcartier or Kandahar—they'll track your cash flow and auto-invest your loose change. Heck, even Reddit forums can be your RECON team, scouting out tips from troops who've already navigated the same financial field.

Here's the rally point—treat your finances like a combat mission. Strategize (budget like you're allocating ammo), optimize (cut the fat, say no to that third gaming console or anything that isn't essential), and advance. You've got a fireteam backing you like mentors, SISIP pros, and this book. Wealth building's a ruck march, not a sprint. Stay disciplined. Hoard every dollar like it's your last ration meal.

Lock and load!

AFTER ACTION REPORT

- **Financial literacy is mission-critical.** Just like tactical readiness, understanding budgeting, saving, and investing is essential for long-term success. Without financial literacy, even high earners can struggle to build wealth.

- **Your mindset is your strongest weapon.** Financial discipline, focus, and accountability are what separate thriving service members from those just getting by. Treat wealth-building like PT—consistent, uncomfortable, but worth it.

- **Every CAF member has millionaire potential.** With the CAF pension as a solid base and smart, strategic planning layered on top, even average earners can retire comfortably and wealthily with the right habits.

- **Set financial goals using a military-grade strategy.** Define your financial mission, break it into OPERA-style goals (Organized, Practical, Effective, Results-driven, Accountable), and prioritize based on urgency and impact.

- **Start where you are—and start now.** Whether you're new to the CAF or halfway through your career, the most important step is beginning. Financial preparedness is non-negotiable, and the sooner you take action, the better your long-term outcome.

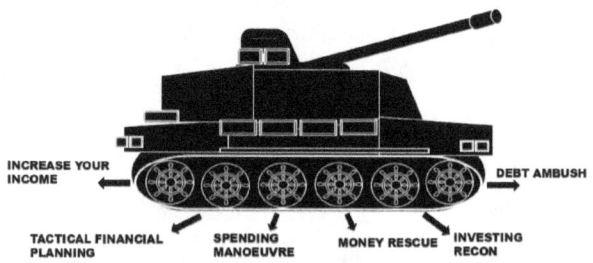

INCREASE YOUR
INCOME

DEBT AMBUSH

TACTICAL FINANCIAL
PLANNING

SPENDING
MANOEUVRE

MONEY RESCUE

INVESTING
RECON

You are richer than you think.
You just need to follow a plan.

DAVID BACH
The Automatic Millionaire

CHAPTER 2

STRATEGIC PLANNING
WEALTH-BUILDING
BLUEPRINT

EVERY SUCCESSFUL MISSION begins with a solid plan. Building wealth is no different. This chapter breaks down the specific steps, roles, and strategies you need to tackle your financial victories. This is my "Wheel of Wealth," a slick tactical approach from my playbook that I've put together to lay the groundwork for securing and growing wealth. Now, let me introduce you to my:

Concept of Operation: Wealth-Building Tactics

Building wealth has nothing to do with luck or shortcuts. It's about staying sharp, playing smart, and most importantly, getting it done. Just as you wouldn't approach a mission without a plan, your finances deserve a deliberate approach. By implementing these proven tactics, you'll strengthen your ability to take control of your finances, shield your financial flank, and achieve long-term prosperity.

Let's dive into each element of the Wheel of Wealth and arm you with the right tools to dominate the financial warzone. Whether you're just starting out or refining your strategy, this set of manoeuvres will help you stay mission ready for every financial challenge ahead. *Copy that? Let's hit the ground!*

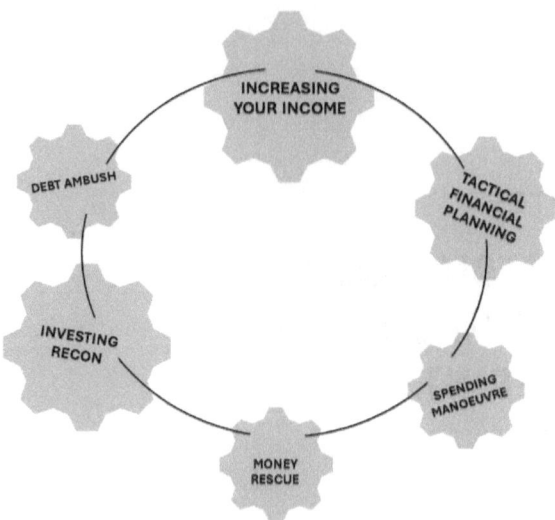

The Wheel of Wealth

CONCEPT OF OPERATION:
WEALTH-BUILDING TACTICS

Consider this your Concept of Operations, a clear, action-able plan to guide you on your mission to wealth building. Just like a CONOP lays out mission steps, each part of the Wheel of Wealth will help you strategize, execute, and adapt to grow wealth. *No cutting corners here!* Follow the plan, stay disciplined, and keep your eyes on the prize. Wealth is built step by step, through savings, smart investments, and strat-egy, just like advancing through mission objectives.

Wealth Fortress

Building a wealth fortress that is tougher than a tank and more resilient than a hardened veteran is about creating a financial stronghold that is set up to smirk at economic storms and keep you rock steady when the world is shaking like a misfired round. To begin, you need a foundation stronger than reinforced steel to shield your cash army. Then, you pile up defences so stout they will laugh at any financial hurricane. Here are the six powerful tactics to dominate the financial battlefield and build an unshakable fortress.

1 **Increasing your income**: expanding your earnings
2 **Tactical financial planning**: setting goals and strategies
3 **Spending manoeuvres**: managing expenses effectively
4 **Money rescue**: saving strategically
5 **Investing recon**: exploring investment options
6 **Debt ambush**: eliminating debt efficiently

Let's dive into each tactic so you're ready to dominate any terrain.

INCREASING YOUR INCOME: EXPANDING YOUR EARNINGS

One of the keys to growing your wealth is to increase your income. You can achieve that by obtaining a higher-paying job or a secondary job. Try starting a side business or investing in your education to improve in a particular field or skills that will potentially bring you more revenue. In other words, expand your earning potential.

More Ammunition

While your CAF salary provides a solid foundation, more money can accelerate your wealth-building efforts. Bringing in extra cash is like calling air support to speed up your wealth-building operations. You need to arm yourself with more than just knowledge and discipline. You need to increase your income with fresh rounds for the battle ahead. That's the heavy arsenal you need. The more that lands in your bank account each month, the more firepower you can allocate toward savings and investments. Resources and strategy drive success, and your financial journey depends on maximizing income and using it wisely. Whether through a secondary job, climbing the ranks for a promotion, or deploying smart investments, every dollar is a bullet for your mag. So, gear up, boost your income, and allocate your resources like a Commander in charge. *Load up your mags!*

Increase Your Firepower

Career advancement within the CAF is your first line of attack. Chase opportunities for promotions, specialized training, or take postings and missions that can lead to higher pay. Take advantage of professional development programs and zero in on roles that sync with your long-term financial goals.

Look into taking on extra work or freelance missions outside of your military duties, leveraging your skills into cash on the side. If you're trained in logistics, you could offer consulting services to small businesses. Maybe you majored in languages, and can teach a French class on the side for extra money. Or, better, if you're tech-savvy, freelance work in IT or web design for your local businesses could provide extra rounds. Just ensure it doesn't interfere with your primary duty and create any conflict of interest with your current position. This can help you diversify your income streams and strengthen your financial stance.

Reload and ramp it up!

Create Passive Stream Income

Passive income is like having a reserve force. It works for you even when you're not actively engaged. Things like dividend-paying stocks (more details on this later), rental properties, digital products (e-books, courses), selling services online, or creating content (travel videos, blogs) can all generate steady income over time. It's like setting up a self-sustaining supply line for your wealth. Once it's in place, it keeps fuelling your financial growth without constant effort. Investments in rental properties, the stock market, or other passive income streams can generate steady returns with minimal effort, allowing you to grow your wealth while staying focused on your primary role: taking care of your CAF duties (more on this in Allocation of Assets).

Without a doubt, boosting your income gives you more ammo to save, invest, and build your wealth. Whether it's through climbing the CAF ladder, side jobs, or pulling extra shifts, the extra rounds will fuel your overall wealth. But to really light the field burners, you need passive income streams. These are like your backup team working for you. Think rental properties, investing, dividend stocks, or digital products you set up once and then watch bring in money over time. Together, increasing your income and adding passive streams let you grow wealth faster and with less day-to-day effort.

Lock it in, troops!

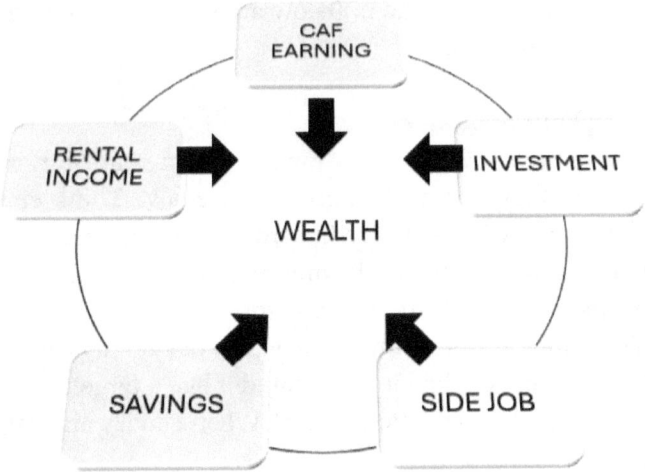

Setting up income streams might feel like a tough, energy-consuming mission. But working forty hours a week until you're sixty-seven? That's a tougher road, if you ask me. And you'll be running on fumes by then. It all comes down to this—you pick your hard (difficulty level); you pick your battle. A little effort now beats decades of exhaustion, and why not choose the path that sets you up for more freedom and a little less struggle?

Choose your hard, soldier!

TACTICAL FINANCIAL PLANNING: SETTING GOALS AND STRATEGIES

To build and grow your wealth, you need a solid plan to confront the financial landscape. Map out a strategy with clear objectives and stick to it. Having a plan and laying it out will help you remain on track. Have an idea of how and where you will allocate every portion of your earnings. Check your position now and then adjust if the Situation Report (SITREP) changes. Tactical financial planning involves setting clear, actionable goals in addition to developing strategies to achieve them. Below are some key steps that helped me succeed.

Setting Your Strategies

Lock in your target—start by pinning down your short and long-term financial goals. Short-term goals? Think emergency fund or wiping out credit card debt. Long-term goals? A house, or retirement. In the military, every mission has an objective; your finances need one too.

For example, one of my goals was to pay off my car loan before my next deployment. I treated it like a target: locked on, disciplined, and mission-critical. When I finally made that last payment, it felt like completing a successful operation. Whatever goals are in your line of sight—write them down.

Create a financial roadmap—break down your goals into actionable steps. Use the OPERA framework discussed earlier to ensure your plan is clear and achievable. For instance, if your goal is to save $10,000 for a down payment for a house, determine how much you need to save each month and adjust your budget accordingly. Tracking your finances is like conducting a RECON mission. You need to know where every buck squad is deployed.

I once had a buddy who couldn't figure out why he was always running out of ammunition (cash). It turns out that he spent $200 a month on energy drinks at the CANEX store. By tracking his expenses, he cut back and saved enough for a down payment on his first home. Lesson learned—keep an eye on your spending, or it'll sneak up on you.

Budget wisely—budgeting is like rationing supplies during a field exercise. You've got to stretch it. I remember a Sergeant who used the 50/30/20 rule: 50% needs, 30% wants or for fun (mostly coffee and candies, he'd laugh), and 20% stashed away in savings. He stuck to his budget and saved enough to take his family to Disney World. Map out your spending, and watch your money carry you further.

Invest smart—investing is like shoring up a strong defence. It guards and grows your wealth. I started putting money aside in a Tax-Free Savings Account (TFSA) and later sprinkled some dividend stocks in it. It felt like earning medals in the market. Those small investments stacked up into a solid stash over time. Start easy, keep to it. (More on TFSA and other tools later!)

Stay locked in—discipline is the backbone of military life and your finances. My old roommate automatically transferred cash to his savings account every payday. He called it his "financial PT," no skipping, and always on schedule. Even when a new PlayStation game tempted him, he held the line. Stay steady, and you'll see results.

Debrief and adapt—like a post-mission rundown, check your financial SITREP regularly. Tweak your plan if pay, bills, or life shift gears. Keep tabs, update as needed, and stay in command. That's how you roll out this operation.

These moves will get you to your financial target. Stay focused, stay disciplined, and remember—every dollar counts. Seek advanced guidance as necessary. The complexity of financial planning can be exhausting and feel like a maze sometimes. When that happens, seek experts' advice.

Those who are victorious plan
effectively and change decisively.

SUN TZU
The Art of War

SPENDING MANOEUVRE: MANAGING EXPENSES EFFECTIVELY

We've touched on how spending habits shape your budget. In our line of duty, resource management is critical to mission success. Your finances run the same way. Effective spending manoeuvres ensure your resources are allocated wisely, leaving room for savings and investments. This portion of the Wheel of Wealth is used to manage your expenses and optimize the use of your hard-earned salary. It typically helps when creating a budget, setting financial goals, and steering money toward essentials while ditching unnecessary purchases. The aim? Make the most of your income, such as reducing debt and saving for the future. Be conscious of your spending patterns to avoid superfluous expenses. You can accomplish this by prioritizing spending on essential items, reducing or eliminating impulse buys, and trimming daily costs. Keep an eye on your budget to stay on course for your financial target. This tightens up your funds as much as possible. Here is how I keep my spending in check:

1   **Track your spending**—start by tracking your expenses for a month. Pinpoint where to trim, such as dining out, subscriptions, or impulse buys.

2   **Need beats want**—distinguish between essential expenses (like housing, groceries, and utilities) and discretionary spending (like entertainment or fancy gear). Dial back on non-essential expenses to free up funds.

3   **Gear up budgeting tools**—leverage budgeting apps or spreadsheets to monitor your cash flow and stay on track.

Slash your expenses and save more money!

What I mean by "slash your expenses" is not to live a frugal lifestyle and avoid all sorts of pleasures in life. What I mean is to budget carefully. Reducing your expenses will help you save more money or kill debt quicker. Check your budget and identify anything that you don't really need, like unused subscriptions or memberships, then cut them. Swap in a cheaper, more cost-effective alternative.

Reduce Subscriptions
- Internet programs
- Magazines
- Online movie subscriptions
- Gym subscription

Alright, listen up! The base gym is free. Sure, it might not be a runway for supermodels or have a sauna, and yeah, it means another hour on base. Maybe it's missing that one fancy machine, but guess what? They've got everything you need to get the job done. And hey, let's be real, are you here to swipe right on a date or to lift some weights and get shredded? *Priorities, people!*

Reduce Discretionary Spending
- Dining in restaurants
- Home deliveries
- Frequent visits to the bars

Fall in! Quit tossing your paycheque on takeout and learn to cook. It's a survival skill that'll save you a fortune. I've seen it. Back in my early days, I had roommates fresh out of basic training who thought "meal prep" meant Domino's on speed dial. By week's end, our place looked like a pizza box bunker. You could've housed a platoon! So, drop the delivery app, grab a spatula, and unleash your inner Gordon Ramsay. Sure, your first attempt might rival the Base kitchen spaghetti, but at least you won't be funding Domino's next corporate retreat. Your bank account and waistline will thank you. *Now, go forth and conquer the kitchen, soldier!*

Manage Your Addiction
- Cigarettes
- Alcohol
- Snacks
- Coffee (more on this one later)

Due to my biological disadvantage, I can't absorb alcoholic beverages or keep up with the pack. Isn't that a twist of fate?

While my buddies are toasting at the mess, I'm over here rocking my soda, living my best life. On the bright side, it's kept my wallet fat over the years. Money straight into my Savings Account and Registered Retirement Savings Plan (RRSP). *Cheers to that!*

Reduce Home Expenses
- Negotiate your mortgage rate
- Rent share
- Downsize your apartment
- Lower the power consumption

Trimming home expenses is like packing light for a mission: less drag, more firepower. Monitor your power usage, cut back on extras, and shrink your housing bills to maximize your monthly savings. I knew a couple who switched to energy-efficient appliances and cut their utility bill by 20%, and diverted that saved cash straight into their car loan. Small changes at home can create big opportunities.

Discount Hunting
- Compare prices across different stores
- Keep an eye out for sales and discounts
- Take advantage of coupons
- Shop at stores with competitive pricing

Squad! Nabbing deals and discounts is like scoring tactical gear at a surplus store; it saves you money, and it's a win, not a weakness. Most folks can't be bothered, but not me. If Costco's gas is ten cents cheaper, I'm rolling in line. That membership card is also a bonus because the cashback means more money in your pocket. Besides, where else can you still find hot dogs and a soda for under $1.50? Inflation never found its way into Costco's snacks. Every buck you save is ammo you can invest in your future. Be smart, be frugal, and watch your savings stack up! Plus, the more you hit Costco, the more you earn back, making Costco your financial ally.

Save on Transportation
- Use public transportation
- Carpool with others
- Drive fuel-efficient vehicles
- Consider driving an electric vehicle (EV)
- Opt for used vehicles

Switching to fuel-efficient transport is like upgrading your gear for a long operation. It's smart, tactical, and a win all around. Giving up the gas-hog ride is like dumping extra weight you don't need. Opting for an electric, a hybrid, or even carpooling, you'll save at the pump and back the green fight. Your piggy bank stays loaded, and the planet scores, too.

Take Sergeant Ecofriendly. She used to drive a massive truck that drank fuel like a recruit chugging water after a forty-kilometre march. She traded it in for a hybrid SUV, slashed fuel costs in half, and banked savings faster than a drill sergeant's push-up count. Plus, she's cutting her carbon footprint, not just her gas bill. *I hear you!* EVs can be pricey, and not everyone can afford rolling up to formation in a Tesla. But technology is moving quickly, and what's expensive today could be affordable tomorrow. So, even if converting to an EV isn't in the cards for you today, no sweat! Carpool, bike, or drive lean instead. Plan ahead, shift when you are ready, and you'll own the road, financially and literally.

Bottom line, cut the fat from expenses, and you'll free up money for the big wins. Less waste means more firepower for your financial mission.

MONEY RESCUE: SAVING STRATEGICALLY

I've been dropping hints about saving money, because let's face it, you can't accumulate wealth without properly saving money. Saving is the backbone of building wealth—it's your reserve unit.

When I say, "save your money," I don't mean that you should live so frugally that you miss out on great experiences in life just to pinch pennies. It's a balancing act. Sure, I am all about maxing out savings, but I also want you to enjoy the ride. And no, I am not saying let it sit in your bank account collecting dust either. "Save more of your money" means stashing your money for more room to invest. More on that soon.

Savings Statistics

According to Statistics Canada, in 2018 the average Canadian household saved just about $850, enough for some basic kit or a month's bill, but that's it. Meanwhile, the top twenty earners stashed around $41,000 per household. That's like maxing out your annual contributions to your savings plan and still having enough left over to take your family for a trip on a Carnival Cruise. By 2020, average savings jumped to $5,800, a huge improvement from the $1,100 average in 2019. That's like going from having barely enough for a weekend pass to saving up for a solid emergency fund. In 2023, households where the primary income earners were aged thirty-five to forty-four recorded the highest net savings, averaging nearly $22,000 Canadian dollars (probably due to the pandemic). But, heads up—even with that improvement, Canadians' savings game is still weak, and this trend will not fix itself soon. Households with individuals aged sixty-five and older experienced net savings of just a little over 13,000 Canadian dollars, indicating that their expenditures exceeded their income. So, what's the mission?

If you're serious about building wealth, be deliberate about your money. Whether it's setting up automatic savings, cutting unnecessary expenses (like that daily coffee run), or investing in your future, it's time to lock in your financial mission and execute. You've got this, now aim it at your vault.

How Much Should You Save?

For savings and retirement, there is no one-size-fits-all, but here's a solid benchmark: George Clason, author of *The Richest Man in Babylon,* suggests a savings rate of 10% of your income.

George Clason Savings Rate

Followed by Dave Ramsey's recommended 15% investment savings rate for retirement.

Dave Ramsey Savings Rate

Then came Elizabeth and Amelia Warren with a popularized 50/30/20 percent method—50% on needs, 30% on wants, and 20% toward savings.

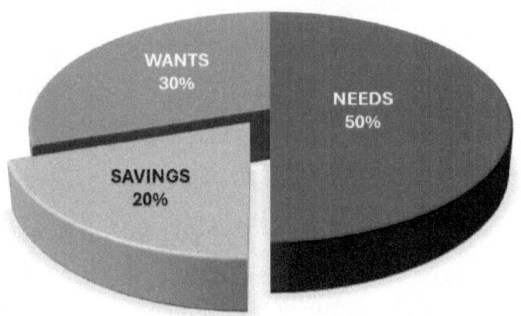

Elizabeth and Amelia Warren Savings Rate

I get it! Everyone and their Commanding Officer (CO) have an opinion on how much you should be saving: 10%, 20%, whatever. We could hash it out all day in the briefing room, but here is the real deal: no matter the percentage, the mission is the same; it gets you to save. Select a rate that fits your kit and works for you, a little or a lot, and stick to it like it's your rifle during inspection.

Here's the scoop (which I'm also saving like it's top-secret intel): why settle for the bare minimum? If you're serious about building wealth and attaining financial independence, like "retire early and never have to slog through another mandatory DND online course again" serious, why stop at 20%? You don't just meet the mark—you crush it, exceed it, and make it happen. Ramp it up to 30%, or more if you are fired up. The way I see it, it's simple: more saving, faster winning. It's like rucking with a lighter load (no need for carrying too much available cash) and hitting the finish line ahead of the pack.

So, step up and crank that savings rate up. It's the mission that sets you up for life after the uniform. Now, go out there and save like your freedom depends on it—*because it does!*

Save as much as you can, while you can!

Achieving your financial goals and retiring early hinges on your savings rate. Ramp up your ammo supply, save more, spend less, and invest more. Those investments pile up over time, filling the gap when your active duty paycheque dries up. Build your stockpile of resources for a lifelong campaign. The higher you push that rate, the faster you'll reach the target. So, aim higher.

Mission: Financial Domination—do you accept it?

Automate Your Savings

Set up automatic transfers to your savings every time you get paid. Lock in your PT schedule on the 15th and the last day of the month as part of your routine when that pay stub kicks in. By having a portion of your cheque automatically moved into savings or investments, you don't have to worry about forgetting or chronic procrastination; *do you follow me?* It's all set up, just like putting your boots on at 0-dark-30 (pitch black). This way, you're consistently building your financial reserves without a second thought.

You can't blow money that you don't have, and by automating the process, you eliminate the temptation to raid your chequing account. It's a set-it-and-forget-it system that keeps you on track without needing constant attention. No more "I'll do it later" nonsense. Automating your savings is an easy win, keeps you disciplined, and compounding interest is reinforced over time. Missing out on those transfers, even a few times, can throw off your financial progress.

I set aside a portion of my income into investments regularly, reload, and repeat, like feeding rounds into a mag. It's low-key, but it's effective. This repetitive process may not seem exciting, but it's a steady one that helps you build real wealth.

How I Save My Ammo (How I Save My Money)

I wasn't always a top-tier saver. In fact, I used to blow through cash like a recruit on their first weekend pass. Then, I wised up, and I got into the habit of living below my means. Swapping meal preps for Michelin-starred meals and quick fast food. I wish I'd started earlier, though. If I had, I'd probably be sipping sugar juice on some beach in Tahiti by now.

I got serious about saving around twenty-eight, which is a solid age to start. Income became more consistent, and I was no longer living paycheque to paycheque. But the real game-changer was discovering the TFSA. At first, I didn't fully grasp its potential, but now? I swear by it like I swear at a dirty microwave in the common area at the unit. I started maxing out my TFSA contributions every year, cutting out frivolous spending (goodbye, monthly subscriptions I forgot I had), and tracking my expenditure. All my extra savings went into that TFSA; then I began investing in stocks. Before I knew it, I'd built a portfolio that was generating passive income.

That TFSA? I treat it like my emergency rations. Strictly off-limits unless it's an actual financial blow-up moment. It's my secret weapon, and every dollar I save is another round in the chamber for building wealth. Whether it's stocks, real estate, or other assets, saving and investing is like stacking ammo for the long war. Start early, remain consistent, and watch your wealth grow. Beyond my TFSA, I have a regular investment account too. I don't keep much cash handy; I just need enough for the essentials (more on TFSA and investment tools in Chapter 3).

This is my preferred savings rate, based on my after-tax CAF salary, deductions, and monthly essential expenses. I set aside 30% to cover my obligations, while the remaining 70% (my unused income) goes directly into my investment account for growth. Note that this rate excludes any returns from my investments and other sources of income.

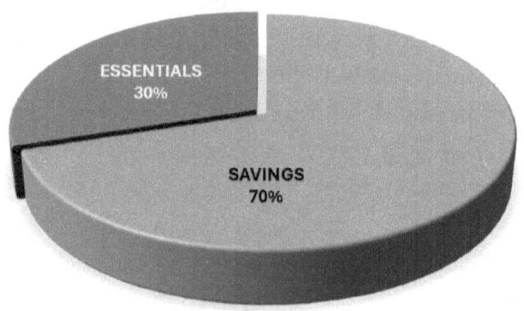

ESSENTIALS
30%

SAVINGS
70%

My Savings Rate

Why Save Money, Troops?

Saving's no optional drill; it's a tactical must. Life is unpredictable, like a last-minute deployment or a random inspection. Building a financial cushion provides you with a backup plan for a mission. It helps you weather storms, stay resilient during tough times, and keep your finances from going Missing in Action (MIA). It's not just hoarding dollars but growing your wealth and loading up for investments. Whether it's a job loss, medical emergencies, or your car deciding to break down at the worst possible hour, start building that buffer now, because money preparedness is your best armour for life's financial defence. Whatever your rank, your income, or your time in service, you must strive to save more money.

That's not advice, it's your marching order.

Fallback Plan (Emergency Fund)

An emergency fund is like your tactical reserve. It's there when the plan goes off script. Whether it's a job loss, a medical bill, or your car breaking down, having a cash reserve keeps you from relying on high-interest debt (aka the greatest enemy). Here's why it's crucial:

- **Job loss**—if you or your partner suddenly loses their job, your emergency fund is your financial parachute, softening the landing.

- **Medical emergencies**—because life doesn't pause for posting season. While serving, we're fortunate to have solid healthcare benefits that cover most needs, but post-service? That shifts. Veteran's Affairs (VA) healthcare might cover some, but out-of-pocket costs, copays, and unexpected medical expenses can still add up fast. A sudden illness, surgery, or long-term care can obliterate your bank account. A medical-ready emergency fund is your lifeline. It ensures you're not scrambling to cover costs or dipping into your retirement savings when the unanticipated happens.

- **Car repairs**—because your ride quitting on you is about as predictable as an old Army Warrant Officer's mood on Monday morning.

Let's bring up a sensitive topic: divorce and separation. In our world, split-ups hit hard and often. How many of you have heard a story about a buddy whose divorce nearly ruined their life and their finances? I'll bet it's more than a few.

Take my colleague. Let's call him "Sergeant Breakup." Breakup was a solid NCM, great at his job, but his personal life was a mess. When his marriage fell apart, he was blind-sided, not just emotionally, but financially. Legal fees, split assets, and suddenly paying for two households emptied his bank account faster than a Private at the CANEX on payday. With no emergency fund, he was forced to rely on credit cards and loans, digging a pit that took years to climb out of. Sound familiar? How many times have you heard a similar story? Divorce is tough enough without adding financial ruin to the mix. But with a solid emergency fund, you can handle the unforeseen costs and keep your head above water.

My Tactical Emergency Fund Breakdown

This is my financial ammo supply, for when life throws a grenade my way. It's designed to cover essentials like:

- Rent/mortgage
- Utilities
- Groceries
- Transportation
- Insurance

Let's break it down further. If you've never saved an emergency fund, anything is better than nothing. But here are a few recommended models:

- **Three months' expenses**—this is your baseline kit, perfect for single members or dual-income households with stable jobs. It's your standard-issued gear. Enough to cover you for a quick fight and get you through short-term chaos.

- **Six months' expenses**—this is the recommended amount for those with dependents, a single-income household, or jobs with less stability (like contractors or reservists, Class A, or Class B). Think of it as packing extra mags for the rifle. It's more firepower to handle bigger challenges, messier battles.

- **Twelve months' expenses**—this is for the advanced-level preppers, those with irregular income, high financial obligations, or who just want to be extra prepared for the apocalypse. It's like having a full supply depot on standby, fully stocked and ready for anything.

So, CAF family, figure out your lane and load up that emergency fund. It's your safety net when the tsunami hits. Because in our world, being prepared is half the fight!

The Timeframe

Alright, CAF warriors! Here is the game plan for building your Tactical Emergency Fund. Here's how to approach it step by step, military fashion:

- **Phase 1—Quick Strike (one to three months).** First up, lock in $1,000 As Soon as Possible (ASAP). This is your "immediate response" fund for small emergencies, like a busted tire or a random bill. Treat it like a high-priority objective. Slash unnecessary spending (no more fancy lattes), offload gear you don't need or grab a side job.

- **Phase 2—Steady Advance (six to twelve months).** Next, aim to save three months' worth of expenses. This is your main assault. Set up auto-transfers from your pay (treat it like a parade square order, no skipping). Use bonuses, tax refunds, or deployment savings to accelerate the pace.

- **Phase 3—Full Fortification (twelve to twenty-four months).** If you're aiming for six to twelve months' worth of expenses, this is your endurance march for the long-term mission. Stay committed.

Let's shine the light on Sergeant Maxfrugal. He's a single NCM with monthly expenses to wrestle, and his goal was to have six months' worth of tossed money ($15,000). Here's how this legend did it:

- **Phase 1**—he saved $1,000 in two months by cutting back on eating out and cancelling unused subscriptions.

- **Phase 2**—he banked $5,000 over the next five months by setting an auto-transfer of $500 straight into his savings account each paycheque.

- **Phase 3**—he sealed the deal at the $15,000 goal in fifteen months by using his tax refund and deployment savings to top it off and call victory.

Now Sergeant Maxfrugal sleeps like a baby on a C-130, knowing he's ready for whatever ambushes lie ahead. Whether it's a surprise relocation to a pricier province, and let's be real, we all know how brutal the cost of living is in British Columbia or Ontario if you've been stationed there. I'm not even talking about housing yet, but you get the picture. New set of winter tires or the car decides to crap out on the road trip. Thanks to his emergency fund, Sergeant Maxfrugal isn't just surviving, he's thriving. Meanwhile, his pal Sergeant Paycheque-to-Paycheque is still sweating over ramen packets after their last move. *Rough time, eh*?

The takeaway for us CAF folks is clear—emergency fund is your reserve ammo. Ready to channel your inner Maxfrugal?

Where do I Keep My Emergency Funds?

Platoon! Your emergency fund isn't for investing. It's for quick access when you need it. I park mine in a high-yield savings account because they offer better interest rates than a standard account. I avoid tying up my emergency fund in stocks, bonds, or other investments. You don't want to be stuck in a financial firefight with no ammo because your money is locked away inside the vault, or your investment has depreciated when you urgently need it.

The CAF Reality

More Money, Yet Still Broke

A well-established CAF member can pull in between $80,000 and $100,000 a year, which sounds like a sweet deal, right? But here's the dynamite—tons of folks are still scraping by even with that kind of earnings. It's wild when you think about it. Compared to other income earners, six figures should mean financial freedom, not struggling to make ends meet. Yet, it's happening all over our ranks, and I'm going to unpack why. This isn't just some random theory—it's the real deal I see every day in the community. It's so common it's almost old news.

Let's set the stage. We'll look at the median household income for CAF members, focusing on the ranks where most people spend the bulk of their careers (and often retire). Think Sergeants and Captains. Some earn less, some earn more. According to Statistics Canada, over half of Canadians are living paycheque to paycheque. The cost-of-living crisis is no joke.

You'd think pulling in $100K would mean smooth sailing, right? More breathing room, more choices, more freedom. But it's not that simple. Take military life as we know it.

One of the perks of being in the military is the challenge of moving around, from coast to coast, new postings, and new adventures for some. It's a blast, a dream come true. But for others, if you have a family, it could turn into a frag grenade. If your spouse isn't in the CAF, every move means they're back to square one. New city, new job hunt, and climbing the ladder again. They might have to take a pay cut, lose benefits, or sometimes can't find work at all. And if they're sidelined for months, it's not just their paycheque that's at stake; it can mess up their career for years.

Let's crunch some numbers. Say you're an officer pulling in $120,000 a year. Sounds great on paper, right, Captain? But if your spouse isn't working, you're effectively covering two people on that salary. Boom, that $120,000 a year feels more like $60,000 each. Now, compare that to a Corporal pulling just over $75,000 a year but with a working spouse. Their household income could easily outpace yours. *Crazy, eh?* The point I am making here is that your salary alone doesn't tell the whole story. Your individual situation, your family, your bills, and your lifestyle matter way more than the number on your pay stub. That's what really shapes the battlefield.

So, what's the play here? If you're making good coin but still tight, it's time to take a hard look at your financial operations. Map out a budget, chop the extra beer runs, and think long game. It's not about how much you bring into your account; it's about what you hang onto and build up. Who else is feeling the pinch?

Forward Operation Base (FOB)

Let's frame this in terms we all get. In combat, a FOB is your lifeline. It provides security and resources when you need them most. An emergency fund serves the same purpose in your financial life. It's your safety net shielding you when life drops a surprise missile round. Aim to build a fund that covers three to six months of living expenses. This is your financial FOB, ensuring you're always prepared for whatever's inbound.

Mission: Financial Peace of Mind, what say you?

INVESTING RECON: EXPLORING INVESTING OPTIONS

Ok, troops! Now we're locking and loading on my favourite segment of the Wheel of Wealth: investing! This is where your money goes from sitting in the barracks to being out there, getting boots on the ground, working hard to build your wealth.

Picture investing like a tactical operation textbook. You gather intel, identify opportunities, and execute a plan to secure your wealth trajectory. By setting aside savings and dropping them into an investment account, you're deploying your resources to achieve a clear path: growing your wealth and generating returns.

Whether you're investing in stocks, bonds, or rental properties, the goal is the same: to increase your asset value or secure a steady income. As the clock ticks, this steady push can bulk up your net worth, stockpile resources for that retirement Landing Zone (LZ), or throw up a financial barricade to handle whatever ambushes life throws your way.

Wealth Building Through Investing

Investing is your ticket to financial independence, but just like any mission, it demands sharp planning and solid preparation. Start by assessing your goals, understanding the risks, and knowing your risk tolerance, kind of like evaluating the terrain before a deployment. Before you send your hard-earned pay into the fray, run some serious reconnaissance. Research the risks and rewards of each investment option and maybe link up with a financial expert to steer you through your opening moves. (Think of them as your financial battle buddy, ok!) I can call a storm several kilometres out, but I am not certified to predict the market like the real professionals, so bringing in experts to back you up is a great move.

Here's a fun fact to keep in mind: Charlie Munger, one of the greatest investors in history, started as a meteorologist before becoming a legend in investing. (May he rest in peace.) He said, *"The wise man looks for what he can learn from everyone."* Whether you're tracking thunderstorms or racking up wealth, before you storm the investing front, take a knee and size up your risk appetite, mission timeline, and financial endgame. Hit the books, call in the professionals for backup, and roll into this money campaign with the same discipline and laser focus you pack in your kit bag. With a rock-solid plan of attack, you can turn your dollars into a powerful asset that pulls its weight as hard as you do.

What to Consider Before Investing

Investing is like drawing up an operation plan. You need a tight strategy, the right gear, and a firm grasp of the battle-field. Here's what I consider:

- **Lock in your objective**—are you saving for retirement, looking to generate passive income, or fund a major purchase? Clear targets steer you to the right playbook, just like setting the NVGs before you deploy.

- **Know your risk threshold**—every investment carries risks, just as every mission has uncertainties. Some stocks are wildcards with big payoffs, while others are stable but grow slowly. Choose investments that align with your comfort level and time horizon.

- **Spread your forces**—don't put all the cartridges in one ammo box. Spread investments across asset classes like stocks, bonds, and real estate. This minimizes losses if one flank takes a hit (underperformed sector). It's like having a fallback position for every scenario.

- **Exercise due diligence**—scout the terrain, understand the companies you invest in, and seek financial intel before deploying your money. Linking up with a financial expert is like having an experienced NCM walk you through the drill.

- **Stay in the fight**—kick it off small and keep it steady. However, invest regularly. You don't need a huge amount to begin. Just like in basic training, start lean, build momentum over time, and watch it roll. Consistent investment piles up, nailing those objectives. This is your pre-deployment Ops checklist.

Ready to map this out!

My Battle Plan Tips

Deploy early—begin building wealth soon. After twenty-five years of service, you'll salute your past self for securing the high ground early. Secure your flank (diversify your portfolio)—spread your investments across different asset classes (stocks, bonds, real estate, etc.) to reduce risk and maximize returns, just like a well-rounded defence system for your wealth. No single threat can breach your wealth's perimeter.

Leverage tax-advantaged accounts—take advantage of accounts like the TFSA or RRSP to grow your investments tax-free or tax-deferred. Use them to shield your gains and advance your position. Stay on mission (this is a long campaign)—wealth building is not a quick operation. Strategize, hold the line with discipline, and let compound growth work like a silent ally. Stay steady, and watch your empire expand.

Ready to move out?

Lessons From My Financial Trenches

When I first started investing, I was practically glued to my command post, eyeballing my account's net value every day and tracking market shifts like it was hot intel rolling in. Watching stock prices bounce around minute by minute turned into my daily drill. And yeah, I still get the rush for daily sneak peaks now and then for a quick SITREP. But back in the early days? I was a shiny new green recruit fumbling through the haze, figuring it out through good trial and error, picking up battle-tested tricks as I went.

When your own money is on the line, the pressure can hit like a mortar round. During a bear market, when stocks take a nosedive, the fear of losing money hits hard and can rattle even the steadiest soldier. That's when you need to lock down your emotional defences tighter than a bunker hatch to avoid panic-selling your investments. On the flip side, don't let FOMO (fear of missing out) push you into chasing a stock just because it's spiking. There is always another shot and more opportunities. Do your research first.

As a rookie investor, you won't have all the SOPs or the full playbook, and that's okay. Lean on the professional before making decisions. That's where SISIP or other financial experts come in. They'll help you hammer out a custom battle plan for your investments that aligns with your goals and how much heat you can handle throughout your financial mission and your career. Picture it like having a trusted

NCM by your side; someone who's been there and seen it all and can help you navigate the financial battlefield with confidence.

In the next chapter, we'll roll into a tactical rundown of your investment arsenal. You'll get the frontline scoop on stocks, bonds, real estate, and other gear to reinforce your investment accounts (portfolio) and hit your mission objectives with pinpoint precision to help you get through the fog of financial war. In the financial battlefield, consistency is your greatest weapon.

It's not the single strike, but the
relentless pursuit that wins the war.

DEBT AMBUSH:
ELIMINATING DEBT EFFECTIVELY

Let's wrap this wealth-building series by facing down the nastiest enemy in the fight: debt! This one will pin you in place faster than a well-laid trap.

Have you ever been in a position where you can't do anything because you are cornered by your financial capability to do more? You feel like you're being chained down a hole and can't dig yourself out? No matter what you do, no matter how hard you try, you end up right where you started. That's debt doing its dirty work. Over time, debt can pile up, often more than a person can handle.

Debt can have a number of significant impacts on CAF members. The constant stress and financial pressure can spark anxiety, depression, and other mental health struggles.

It can make even the basics, like food, housing, or saving for tomorrow, feel out of reach. Forget about saving for tomorrow when you are barely surviving today. In extreme cases, it spirals into bankruptcy, torching everything you've built. But it doesn't stop with you; others get caught up in the blast radius. High levels of debt ripple outward, straining bonds with family, friends, and especially your life partner. If left unchecked, it can derail your financial mission and your life, blocking your path to the goals you've set. Tackling debt early and managing it well isn't just about money, but breaking free and keeping your future in your crosshairs.

Ticking Bomb

Let's face it! Debt is like a ticking bomb strapped to your financial future. The longer you carry it, the more interest stacks up, and the louder that ticking gets. Next thing you know, you're stuck in a financial minefield, dodging interest charges and watching your dreams of a debt-free life explode. *But hold tight, troops!* this section is your bomb squad disposal manual. We are going to disarm that one together and get you clear. *Ready to cut the wires?*

Tik, Tik, Tik, Tik, Tik . . .

Tackle your debt ASAP before it
becomes a much greater nuisance.

Why is debt your most fearful enemy? Debt is like that one recruit who always shows up late to formation. It's annoying, it slows you down, screwing up the entire platoon. It just makes everything harder. The longer you let it hang around, the more it costs you. High-interest debt, like credit card debt, is the worst offender.

Imagine you're on a mission, and your squad is carrying way too much gear. Every step feels heavier, and you're moving at a snail's pace. That's what debt does to your finances: it weighs you down and limits your ability to make other moves, like saving for a house or investing for retirement. Debt is the enemy you *SHALL* not ignore.

Tackle Your Debt ASAP

Debt doesn't just drain your capital bunker—it'll kneecap your credit score, making it a nightmare to get a loan for that dream home or even a half-decent car. And really, no one wants to explain to their kids why they can't go to the movies or take a family vacation because you are still paying off that "emergency" fishing boat purchase from three years ago.

Need tactical insight? Paying off debt is like sweeping a minefield. You've got to move carefully, but once the ground has cleared, you've got a safe path to your financial objectives. Clear your debt ASAP!

Debt Control

Dealing with debt is like running a crucial operation. You need a killer plan, the right gear, and some serious backbone. Here's my debt mission brief, straight from my playbook. *Ready for your orders?*

- **Create a budget**—think of your budget as your mission map. It shows you where your money is going and where you need to cut back. Maybe you don't need that daily eight-dollar latte from the nearby base coffee shop. (Yes, you, Tim Hortons and Starbucks addict.) A buddy of mine realized he was spending $200 a month on energy drinks. He switched to water, saved that cash, and used it to pay off his credit card. Now he's debt-free and, ironically, has more energy.

- **Prioritize your debts**—not all debts are created equal. High-interest debts, like credit cards, are the enemy's heavy artillery. Take them out first. Lower-interest debts, like student loans, can wait their turn. Use the "debt avalanche" method: focus on the debt with the highest interest rate first while making minimum payments on the others. It's like taking out the enemy's command post before mopping up the stragglers.

- **Consolidate your debts**—if your debts are spread out like foot soldiers in the field, consider consolidating them into one loan with a lower interest rate. It's like calling in reinforcements to simplify your battle plan. Another colleague consolidated her credit card debts into a single personal loan with a lower interest rate. She saved hundreds in interest.

- **Negotiate with creditors**—sometimes, you've got to talk to the enemy. Call your creditors and negotiate a better payment plan or a lower interest rate. It's like brokering a ceasefire. Every little bit helps. For example, take Sergeant Ironjaw, whose credit card debt had hit DEFCON 1 (the highest alert level in the US military's Defence Readiness Condition). With a 29% interest rate, the $15K balance was advancing faster than an enemy blitz. Instead of retreating, Sergeant Ironjaw launched a counter-operation. He dialled the creditor's headquarters armed with his service record and a clear objective: negotiate terms or threaten to transfer the balance to a 0% card (his backup platoon). Result? After thirty minutes of tactical diplomacy, citing his steady military paycheque and loyalty, the creditor agreed to a ceasefire—a 9% interest rate and frozen fees. His family's net savings: $300/month, redeployed to his emergency fund.

- **Ramp up your revenue**—when you're outgunned, sometimes you need to request tactical support. Taking on a side hustle, like driving for a ride-share service or selling unused gear online, can give you the extra firepower to tackle your debt. I once took a part-time job delivering Thai food to pay off a credit card. Was it glamorous? No. Did it work? Absolutely. And hey, free Pad Thai.

- **Seek professional help**—if the debt bomb is too big to handle alone, call in the experts. SISIP offers free financial counselling to CAF members. I've used their services myself, and they're like the special forces of debt management. I've deployed their intel during tight operations, and they're elite at cutting through red tape and strategizing exits. I also rallied my banking institution's advisers (allies with firepower) to renegotiate rates and consolidate loans. More boots on the ground equals fewer blind spots.

Paying off debt isn't easy or quick. It's a tactical advance under pressure. Marching through hostile terrain, inch by inch, suppressing threats as you go. You've got to keep putting one foot in front of the other. But once you're debt-free, you'll celebrate on high ground. You'll have more money, more freedom, and more options to conquer your next mission.

The only easy day was yesterday.
Tackle your debt today, and
your future self will thank you.

The Coffee Compound Effect

Small indulgences, big expenses. Those little treats sneak up on you. The military personnel appreciate their coffee, don't they? I am right there too, guilty as charged! In fact, before beginning my day, I yearn for a steamy and delicious cup of freshly brewed coffee to kick off my day. There is no better way to tackle the world's problems than with a cup of coffee. Nothing is as comforting as the aroma of coffee beans, a whiff of cilantro, and the warm, well-worn scent of old books. That's my happy place.

Some of the biggest coffee names are conveniently camped near every base. Just look for your closest CANEX stores, and bam, there is a Tim's Horton next door, if not right inside. Feeling rich or fancy right after payday? Starbucks is not too far away either. Me? It's McDonald's Coffee! Every morning, chances are that you'll see a good lineup circling around the coffee chain near your base—people waiting in line to get their dose of that dark, liquefied gold before heading into work.

I bring this up to highlight how those small daily splurges, like that daily cup of coffee, can add up over time. It feels like pocket change at first, but it's a ninja, quietly ballooning into a hefty tab. What seems insignificant at first can quietly snowball into a substantial expense. By month's end, those little indulgences can leave you with a much larger bill than you'd expect, nibbling away at your hard-earned money without you even realizing it. It's the reverse compound effect in action. Small moves, big damages.

Who else is hooked on the coffee run?

The CAF's Love Affair with Coffee

After years of observing my colleagues and their coffee habits (yes, I've basically become a caffeine detective), I've gathered some eye-opening results that I'm about to share with you. Believe it, you'll be shocked at how much one person can spend on coffee alone.

At the time of writing this, the average cost of a medium coffee is around $2.50. As of 2024, that's about the average cost of a standard medium cup of coffee, and in major Canadian cities, this could vary depending on the brand and location. Here's a general breakdown:

- **Canadian average cost**: $2.29 to $2.50 for a medium coffee.

- **City-specific averages**: Toronto, Vancouver, and Montreal prices tend to be on the higher end due to higher living costs, with Starbucks and independent cafés charging closer to $3.00 for specialized coffee.

- **Calgary, Ottawa, Edmonton**: Prices are slightly lower, with Tim Hortons and Starbucks averaging $2.50 to $3.50.

- **Independent cafés average cost**: $3.50 to $5.00 for a medium coffee, depending on the location and specialty offerings.

Take our famous Corporal Bloggings (name changed to protect the coffee-addicted). This individual rolled into work every day with a large "two creams, two sugars" in hand, five days a week, without fail. And on those long shifts? Sometimes it was two cups a day. And let's not even get started on the occasional donuts or energy drinks that tagged along. I decided to crunch the numbers to see just how much this daily ritual was costing. For simplicity, we'll stick to the coffee. Here's how it added up.

AVERAGE COFFEE SPEND		
TIME PERIOD	**CUPS OF COFFEE**	**TOTAL SPEND**
WEEK	5 cups	$12.50
MONTH	20 cups	$50.00
YEAR	240 cups	$600.00

How a Small Cup of Coffee Can Fund Your Future

We can arguably debate how a small cup of coffee could hinder your wealth-building endeavours. Let's settle the debate once and for all. Can skipping that daily $2.50 cup of coffee really make a difference in your wealth-building journey? Spoiler alert—yes, it can. I am about to drop some numbers that'll smack you harder than a 5 a.m. group workout.

The Coffee Math

Imagine this, instead of buying a $2.50 coffee every day, fifty per month (because let's be real, most of us aren't stopping at just one cup). If you invest that $50 every month for twenty-five years at an annualized interest rate of 8%, here's what happens:

- **Your total contributions**: $15,000 (that's 50 x 12 months x 25 years).

- **Your cumulative interest**: $32,918.33 (thanks to the magic of compound interest).

- **Your total value after 25 years of service**: $47,918.33.

And that's only with an average return of 8% on a $2.50 coffee cup. So, yes, frequent spending on expensive coffee can hinder your financial growth over time.

YEAR	MONTHLY INVESTMENT 8%	TOTAL CONTRIBUTION	CUMULATIVE INTEREST	TOTAL VALUE
1	$50	$600	$25	$625
5	$50	$3,000	$1,469	$4,469
10	$50	$6,000	$7,401	$13,401
15	$50	$9,000	$17,230	$26,230
20	$50	$12,000	$32,071	$44,071
25	$50	$15,000	$32,918	$47,918

THE CUP OF COFFEE INVESTMENT FUND

Note: This amount could be higher due to rising costs

Here's the combat assault. This isn't just about that coffee habit. This principle applies to every little repeat offender in your budget. That $10 lunch you grab daily? Redirect that sum into investments, add twenty-five years, and you are looking at over $287,000. That subscription service you never use. Cutting it could add thousands to your future wealth. So, next time you're tempted to grab that coffee, energy drink or snack, hit pause and ask yourself—is this worth $48,000? Because that's what you're potentially giving up.

My frontline guidance! Ease on that. You don't need to give up all your guilty pleasures cold turkey. Instead, try redirecting a portion of those everyday splurges into investments. You'll be surprised at how quickly those small contributions grow over time. Building wealth isn't about gutting your life; it's about making smart choices with the small stuff. Little sacrifices.

So, sip that favourite brew (consider brewing it at home this time), and start channelling those mini expenses into something that grows (investments). Every little bit counts!

Wealth isn't built by quitting life—
it's built by rethinking the little things.
Brew smart. Spend wise. Grow steady.

AFTER ACTION REPORT

- **Diversify your income sources to boost wealth building.** The Wheel of Wealth framework will enhance your cash flow by exploring various sources of income or upskilling opportunities to pursue higher-paying roles within the CAF or beyond.

- **Setting goals, saving money and tracking progress are key.** Define your specific financial objectives, save as much as possible, create a detailed budget, and invest those savings wisely. This approach is key to building and growing your wealth.

- **Create a financial safe bunker before it becomes critical.** Begin with a modest emergency fund and gradually expand it to cover a larger portion of expenses for an extended period. Automate your savings for effective results.

- **Spend purposefully to avoid negative progress.** Monitor every dollar, reduce discretionary spending, and avoid lifestyle inflation. Eliminate excess and prioritize what truly adds value, and remove financial distractions.

- **Engage debt aggressively before it compounds.** Focus on eliminating debt. List your debts, prioritize high-interest ones, and apply the snowball or avalanche method.

*The most important thing about
investing is to get the basic right.*

JIM ROGERS
A Gift to My Children

CHAPTER 3

RECONNAISSANCE
COLLECTING
INTELLIGENCE
ON INVESTMENTS

WE'VE LAID DOWN a solid foundation in the previous chapters. Now it's time to level up and advance to the next phase of your wealth-building mission: mastering the art of investing. Grab your notepads, troops, this is intel you'll need to capture. This marks a pivotal step in your wealth-building strategy, where you'll learn to collect and grow your resources through disciplined and strategic investment moves. Done right, investing has consistently proven to be one of the most powerful ways to achieve long-term financial stability and success, much like a well-planned mission ensures victory.

Just as you wouldn't deploy without reconnaissance and a solid plan, investing demands preparation and strategy. Understanding investment types is like studying the battlefield. It equips you to make calls that align with your financial goals. In this chapter, we'll break down the key components of successful investing, including:

1   Understanding the Battlefield: Types of Investments
2   Risk Assessment: Risk Tolerance
3   Be on Alert: Understanding the Financial Landscape

This chapter will empower you to approach investing with the same precision and focus as a mission-critical operation.

UNDERSTANDING THE BATTLEFIELD: TYPES OF INVESTMENTS

In this section, we'll explore common types of investments that can help you grow your wealth, along with the basics of how each one works. This includes:

- Stocks
- Bonds
- Mutual funds & ETFs
- Real estate

Stocks: The Offensive

Stocks represent ownership in a company, placing you on the frontline of its financial operations. When you buy stocks or shares of a company, you're essentially acquiring a stake in that business. Think of investing in stocks as planting seeds for a thriving financial forest. Over time, as the company grows and becomes more profitable, the value of your shares can rise, and this process is known as capital appreciation.

But there's more. Many companies reward shareholders with dividends, like bonus rations, or the fruits of your investment tree. These regular payouts can be reinvested to accelerate wealth growth through compound interest, allowing you to earn returns on your returns.

Stocks can offer significant growth potential but, heads up, they also come with increased risk. Their value fluctuates based on the company's performance and market conditions, like how a mission can pivot based on new intelligence. Here is the short rundown on two primary types of stocks:

1 **Common Stocks**—these provide shareholders with voting rights and the potential for dividends, which are payments made to shareholders from a company's profits.

2 **Preferred Stocks**—these, generally, do not offer voting rights but provide fixed dividends and a higher claim on assets in the event of liquidation (when the company goes bankrupt and its assets are sold off).

Here are some of the top stocks on the S&P 500, as well as the most valuable companies based on their market capitalization:

S&P 500 MOST VALUABLE COMPANIES		
COMPANIES	MARKET CAP	TICKER
1 NVDIA (Technology)	$2.94 T	NVDA
2 MICROSOFT (Technology)	$2.86 T	MSFT
3 APPLE (Technology)	$3.18 T	AAPL
4 TESLA (Technology)	$791 B	TSLA
5 AMAZON (Technology)	$2.09 T	AMZN
6 ALPHABET (Technology)	$2.0 T	GOOGL
7 META (Technology), formerly Facebook	$1.53 T	META
8 UNITEDHEALTH GROUP (Healthcare)	$444 B	UNH
9 EXXON MOBIL (Energy)	$480 B	XOM

Data as of February 2025

These stocks are some of the largest and most influential companies in the US, contributing significantly to the performance of the S&P 500 index (500 most valuable companies based on market capitalization). By understanding the dynamics of stocks and their potential rewards and risks, you can make informed decisions that align with your financial goals and risk tolerance.

Bonds: The Defensive

Bonds serve as the support units in your investment strategy, offering stability and dependability. When you invest in bonds, you're essentially lending money to a government or corporation. In return, you receive periodic interest payments and the return of the bond's face value when it matures. Bonds are generally considered safer than stocks and provide a predictable income stream, making them an excellent tool for balancing risk in your portfolio. Here are the main types of bonds:

1   **Government Bonds**—issued by national governments, these are often regarded as low-risk investments. For example, in Canada, you can invest in Government of Canada bonds, which are backed by the federal government and are considered one of the safest investment options available.

2   **Corporate Bonds**—issued by companies, these bonds carry a higher risk compared to government bonds but also offer the potential for higher returns. The risk level depends on the financial health of the issuing company, with more stable corporations offering lower yields and riskier companies providing higher yields to attract investors.

By mixing bonds into your investment strategy, you can create a more balanced and diversified portfolio, reducing overall risk while still generating steady returns. Whether you prioritize safety with government bonds or seek higher returns with corporate bonds, understanding these instruments is also a key to building a resilient financial plan.

Mutual Funds and ETFs: Joint Operations

The Tactical Team (Mutual Fund)

Mutual funds function like a well-coordinated tactical team, pooling money from multiple investors to purchase a diversified portfolio of stocks, bonds, or other securities. This approach allows for risk diversification and professional management, making it easier for individual investors (like you) to access a broader range of investments without needing to conduct extensive reconnaissance on each one. Key points about mutual funds:

1 **Diversification**—by investing in a mix of assets, mutual funds reduce risk. This is akin to having various units cover different sectors of the battlefield, minimizing the impact if one area encounters difficulty.

2 **Management**—managed by financial professionals, mutual funds can be an excellent choice for those who prefer not to actively manage their investments. They let you focus on your daily job.

The Agile Operative (ETF)

Finally, ETFs combine the best of both worlds. They operate like stocks, trading on exchanges throughout the day, while offering the diversification benefits of mutual funds, often with lower fees. ETFs are an excellent choice for service members or anyone seeking a flexible, cost-effective way to invest in a broad range of assets. They provide an easy entry point into diversified investing, making them ideal for those who may relocate frequently, do not have significant time to allocate to studying and continuously following the market, or prefer a more hands-on approach to managing their portfolio.

One of the key advantages of ETFs is their variety. They can track specific indices (like the S&P 500), focus on sectors (such as technology, banking, or healthcare), or even follow commodities (like gold or oil). This allows you to invest in a wide range of markets and sectors without the need to pick individual stocks, simplifying the process while still offering exposure to growth opportunities.

Whether you're looking for broad market exposure, sector-specific investments, or commodity-based strategies, ETFs provide a versatile and efficient way to build a diversified portfolio tailored to your financial goals. Here are a few examples:

- **XIU—iShares S&P/TSX 60 Index ETF**: Tracks the performance of the sixty largest companies on the Toronto Stock Exchange (TSX).

- **VCN—Vanguard FTSE Canada All Cap Index ETF**: A broad-based ETF that tracks the performance of Canadian stocks across various market caps.

- **ZEB—BMO Equal Weight Banks Index ETF**: Provides exposure to the largest Canadian banks by equally weighting the stocks of the big six banks: Royal Bank of Canada, TD Bank, Scotiabank, BMO, CIBC, and National Bank.

- **XAW—iShares MSCI All Country World Index ex Canada ETF**: Provides exposure to global equities, excluding Canadian stocks.

- **HAL—Horizons Canadian Dividend ETF**: Focuses on Canadian companies with a strong track record of paying dividends.

Gathering intelligence on various investment types is vital for a successful mission. By understanding stocks, bonds, mutual funds, and ETFs, you can formulate a robust investment strategy tailored to your financial goals and military lifestyle. Equip yourself with this knowledge, and you'll be better prepared to traverse the economic landscape with confidence and precision.

Real Estate: The Stronghold

This strategy can be a game-changer for building wealth, especially if executed thoughtfully. Over the course of a twenty-five-year military career, you'll likely be posted to multiple locations, each offering a unique opportunity to invest in real estate. Whether it's purchasing your first home or acquiring an investment property, real estate can serve as a powerful wealth-building tool. After four or five years (average duration of a posting), your property could appreciate significantly, but the benefits extend far beyond just value appreciation. Here's why real estate is a smart move for CAF members:

- **Property appreciation**—your home's value can increase over time, especially in high-demand areas (close to major Canadian Bases).

- **Building equity**—every mortgage payment builds your ownership stake in the property.

- **Personal accomplishment**—there's pride in owning a home and creating a space that's truly yours.

- **Passive income potential**—rent out all or part of your property or sell it for a profit down the line.

Property Appreciation

Back in 2015, I bought my first home in Saint John, New Brunswick. At the time, I wasn't thinking about turning the house for a profit or making a big financial move. I just wanted a place to call my own. But as life often does, it found a way to throw me a curveball. Eight months in, I ended up selling that house for 60% more than what I paid. It felt like winning the lottery, and at that moment, it became a turning point in my financial journey.

In the midst of chaos, there is also opportunity.

SUN TZU
The Art of War

Here's the back story—I was going through a breakup, and living an hour away from work started to feel impractical and sucked the life out of me. The daily commute was draining my time, energy, and wallet. Around the same time, I noticed something interesting. Houses in my neighbourhood were selling for significantly higher prices than usual. *Lightbulb moment!* I saw an opportunity and decided to list my home.

The response was almost immediate. Within three days, I had an offer just $3,000 shy of my asking price. A week later, it was a done deal. I walked away with a substantial profit, and it completely changed how I thought about real estate and financial opportunities.

Looking back, I learned a valuable lesson: timing and market trends matter in real estate. If I hadn't been paying attention to what was happening in my local real estate market, I might have missed that opportunity altogether. For us military members, this hits home. During posting season, demand for housing often spikes, creating a prime environment for selling if the stars align.

That whole experience taught me to always keep an eye on the market, stay adaptable, and be ready to act when the right opportunity arises. It wasn't just a financial win; it rewired my brain. Real estate isn't just about having a roof over your head; it's a powerful weapon for building wealth, especially in a lifestyle as mobile as the military.

Since then, I've carried those lessons with me every step of the way, and they've shaped how I approach every financial decision. Whether it's property or other investments, I've learned that being informed, proactive, and strategic can turn even the most unexpected situations into goldmines of opportunities and growth.

Seize your next break, soldier!

Building Equity

When you own a home, every mortgage payment builds equity. It's your ownership stake in the property. Think of it as a forced savings plan. Over time, as you pay down your mortgage and your home's value increases, your equity grows. Let's say you buy a house for $400,000. After a few years, your home's value increases to $500,000, and your equity is now $170,000 (assuming $100,000 in appreciation value + your initial contribution of $50,000 + your payment of $20,000). This equity can be leveraged for future investments, like buying a second property or funding renovations to increase your home's value even further.

Personal Accomplishment

Owning a piece of land or a home you can call your own is more than just a financial investment. It's a source of pride and a potential legacy for future generations. There's something deeply satisfying about having a place that's truly yours, a tangible symbol of your hard work and success. For many, a home is the most expensive purchase they'll ever make, and the sense of accomplishment that comes with it is incredibly rewarding.

However, as a CAF member, the reality of frequent postings adds a layer of complexity to homeownership. Unless you're one of the rare few who stay in one location for your entire career (which, let's be honest, is about as likely as finding a perfectly pressed uniform after a field exercise), you'll likely be moving every four to five years. This doesn't mean you shouldn't buy a home; it just means you need to approach it strategically depending on your situation.

Passive Income Potential

Owning a rental property can be like establishing a FOB; it generates steady income and strengthens your financial position without requiring constant oversight. Rent payments from tenants create regular cash flow, turning your property into a source of passive income that can grow your wealth significantly over time.

Real estate isn't just a place to live, it's a strategic asset. Investing in high-growth areas, like near a CFB or a developing community, can boost your property's value through the years, much like a well-executed mission delivers compounding results. While maintenance costs are part of the deal, they're small compared to the long-term gains.

The tactical advantage? Even if you don't sell, you can tap into your property's equity to fund other investments, start a business, or achieve your financial goals. Think of it as having a reserve unit ready to deploy when opportunities arise. In a rising market, real estate becomes a cornerstone of your financial strategy, offering both stability and growth potential. Property appreciation is like holding a key position, and it gains value with minimal effort.

Whether you're building equity, generating rental income, or leveraging your investment, real estate is a powerful tool in your wealth-building arsenal.

Posting Season Opportunity

Master-Corporal (MCpl) Moovalot purchased a house in 2020 for $420,000 at an interest rate of 2.34% (just before the interest rate hikes) and a down payment of 20%.

By the time MCpl Moovalot sold the house in 2023, the member had made nearly $395,000 in profit. Subtract $84,000 for the initial down payment, and it's just above $311,000 clear in the member's pocket.

	HOUSE PRICE APPRECIATION			
	2020	**2021**	**2022**	**2023**
PRICE	$420,000			$700,000
DOWN PAYMENT	$84,000 (20%)			
MORTGAGE BALANCE (2.34%)	$336,000 (Initial)	$325,130 (+12 Months)	$315,715 (+24 Months)	$305,213 (+36 Months)

In the early stages of your military career, buying a home can feel like setting up camp in a hurricane. You might get posted to a new CFB, barely unpack your Furniture and Effects (F&E), and bam, new orders come in and you are boxing up again, heading to the other side of the country. But here's the flip side: each posting is an opportunity to cash in. Each time you sell, you create more wealth that adds up to your overall personal net worth.

Need more convincing? Here are some other reasons why real estate investing works for CAF members:

- **Frequent moves = frequent opportunities**—each posting is a chance to buy, sell, or rent property.

- **Stable income**—your CAF salary makes you an attractive candidate for mortgages.

- **Forced savings**—building your equity through mortgage payments is like paying yourself first.

- **Market knowledge**—living in different regions gives you insight into local real estate trends.

- **Flexible financing options**—many lenders (Banque of Montreal, BMO) offer specialized mortgage products tailored to CAF members, making it easier to secure a loan even with frequent relocations.

- **Tax benefits**—homeownership can bring various tax advantages, including deductions for mortgage interest and property taxes, which can benefit CAF members in different financial situations.

- **Building long-term wealth**—real estate investments can appreciate over time, providing CAF members with a way to build wealth and potentially secure financial stability after their service.

- **CAF relocation benefits**—buying a house as a CAF member is a secret weapon, a secret coupon book. This is your golden ticket to saving cash. Check this out! First off, say bye-bye to lawyer fees and land transfer taxes. That's right! Those heavy costs are totally wiped out! That's an easy $1,000 if not more saved right there. Oh, and all those other random closing fees? They'll probably ghost you too, putting a couple thousand back in your pocket. Cha-ching, right? For detailed information on relocation benefits, please refer to the CAF regulations relevant to your specific situation.

RISK ASSESSMENT: RISK TOLERANCE

Risk comes from not
knowing what you're doing.

WARREN BUFFETT

Figuring out your risk tolerance is crucial in selecting the right investments that fit you, as stocks can experience significant fluctuations influenced by factors like economic shifts, corporate performance, or global events. For instance, during the COVID-19 pandemic between 2020 and 2021, many stocks tanked, reminding us of the unpredictability of markets. Just as reconnaissance is necessary to understand the battlefield, investors must understand the forces that drive stock price fluctuations. These factors, while unpredictable, are part of the landscape, much like the changing terrain a soldier faces in the field.

Your investment horizon and time in the market are also critical. Like a soldier preparing for a long mission, you must be ready for short-term challenges and avoid reacting impulsively during market declines. In the military, you know that setbacks are part of the journey, but this doesn't mean you have to abort the mission. The mission continues. Similarly, in investing, staying focused on the long-term goal will help you avoid the temptation to withdraw prematurely. Patience, discipline, understanding the companies you want to invest in, and your financial strategy to tackle the storm are key to enduring the volatile market and hitting your target.

BE ON ALERT: UNDERSTANDING THE FINANCIAL LANDSCAPE

The presence of danger has a
way of making you feel fully awake.

TIM O'BRIEN
The Things They Carried

You wouldn't step into an operation without knowing the lay of the land, the enemy, and your mission. Investing is no different. The intel and financial landscape are important. It's how you load information to make killer, strategic decisions. Without it, you're essentially going into the mist blind. A risk you can't afford to take. Knowledge is your greatest weapon, and staying informed is your financial armour. Start by following trusted financial news, analyzing company reports, and tracking key economic indicators like interest rates, inflation, and employment data. Consider these your "market reconnaissance." They provide the intel you need to navigate the financial landscape. This habit won't just help you spot opportunities and sharpen your financial skills; it'll also make you a pro at understanding the economy. And let's be honest, it's a great way to liven up conversations.

Imagine casually dropping market insights at a social gathering and suddenly, you're the most intriguing person in the room (and not just the one who knows every military fact by heart). It might even open unexpected doors. Tools like stock screeners and investment apps can act as your "mission control," helping you analyze trends and identify opportunities. But remember, the financial world is full of noise, sensational headlines, market hype, and conflicting opinions. Stay focused on your personal long-term goals.

I learned this the hard way early on. I jumped on a "hot stock tip" without research and paid the price, literally. That mistake taught me the value of discipline and sticking to my strategy, no matter how tempting it is to stray. Stay sharp, stay informed, and watch your knowledge and opportunities grow.

AFTER ACTION REPORT

- **Educating yourself on investment opportunities will help you make informed investing decisions.** Explore stocks for growth, bonds for stability, or real estate for long-term gains, each with a varying level of risk, return, and accessibility.

- **Understanding your financial limits is key to a solid foundation.** Choose an investment that matches your unique financial profile, whether you are cautious or aggressive. Carefully select assets that align with your time horizon and goals.

- **Stay attuned to market conditions for smarter moves.** Monitor trends, economic shifts, global events, and local changes that affect your investments. This will enable you to adapt your strategies proactively as needed.

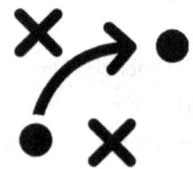

*The key to success
is action, and the essential
in action is perseverance.*

SUNIL MITTAL
billionaire entrepreneur

CHAPTER 4

TACTICAL EXECUTION
DEPLOYING INVESTMENT STRATEGY

IN THIS SECTION, we'll break down the steps to get your investment strategy off the ground and running. Before a mission, you need to set up your command centre, which means opening the right investment accounts and strategically deploying your resources. We'll lay out a clear timeline to stay on course and highlight why it's crucial to track progress and tweak things as you go. Here are the five key steps to set your financial strategy in motion:

1 Identifying a Command Centre: Investment Vehicles
2 Making The First Move: Open Your Investment Accounts
3 Asset Allocation: Deploying Your Resources
4 Establishing a Tactical Timeline: The Financial Campaign
5 Monitoring Operations: Regular Review

Whether contributing to an RRSP, buying stocks, or exploring real estate, each move builds your wealth. The goal? Get your cash to work as hard as you do, turning your money into a loyal ally.

Ready to take action?

IDENTIFYING A COMMAND CENTRE:
INVESTMENT VEHICLES

Financial expert Peter Lynch said it best:

It's not just how much you earn,
but how much you save and invest that
shapes your future prosperity.

Investing is like preparing for a big task. It demands planning, a strategic approach, and the ability to roll with changes. The key for us Canadians? Identifying and choosing the right investment tools (TFSAs, RRSPs, brokerage accounts, etc.) to get the job done. Every successful mission starts with a well-established command centre, where all decisions, strategies, and resources are coordinated for maximum impact. That's what your finance base is here for. It's a setup step where you choose the accounts to hold and grow your wealth. By carefully selecting the right tools, you ensure that your investments are working as efficiently as possible.

For military personnel, who often face unique challenges like deployment, frequent moves, and inconsistent income (spousal income reduction, parental leave, etc.), choosing the right investment accounts can make a significant difference in building long-term wealth. Here is my take on the best options, and how well they can help you save, invest smartly, and maximize your contribution toward building wealth in the most effective way possible:

A TFSA

B RRSP

C Brokerage Accounts (Non-Registered Accounts)

D First Home Savings Account (FHSA)

Investment Vehicles

A. TFSA

This is a powerful tool for military members looking to grow their wealth tax-free. That's right! This tactical advantage on the financial battlefield will maximize your resources without worrying about unnecessary obstacles, just as you'd utilize your environment to gain the upper hand in a mission. With a TFSA, any earnings and profits from investments, whether they're interest, dividends, or capital gains, stay tax-free, making it a valuable resource for accumulating wealth over a long period of time.

For someone in the Forces, the TFSA can act as a flexible savings account that grows without tax headaches, whether you're setting up a future goal or investing in retirement.

TFSA CONTRIBUTION LIMITS		
YEAR	ANNUAL LIMIT	CUMULATIVE LIMIT
2009 to 2012	$5,000	$20,000
2013 to 2014	$5,500	$31,000
2015	$10,000	$41,000
2016 to 2018	$5,500	$57,500
2019 to 2022	$6,000	$81,500
2023	$6,500	$88,000
2024 to 2025	$7,000	$102,000

Government of Canada—TFSA Contribution Room

B. RRSP

The RRSP is another essential tool, particularly for those planning for retirement. With RRSPs, contributions are tax-deferred, meaning you get immediate tax relief by deducting your contributions from your taxable income. That's a handy perk for military personnel who may want to lower their taxable income in the short term. The RRSP also helps build retirement wealth, with earnings growing tax-free until withdrawal.

By the time you retire with a reduced income, you'll have the flexibility to withdraw a portion of your funds in a calculated manner, timing it to keep more in your pocket, ensuring maximum returns. This approach enables you to benefit from growth over the years and provides a valuable supplement to your income during your later years when earnings are more limited.

C. Brokerage Accounts (Non-Registered Account)

While TFSAs and RRSPs are great for tax benefits, brokerage accounts give you the flexibility to invest without limits on contributions or withdrawals. These are ideal for military personnel who might need to access funds quickly or want to invest more freely. Brokerage accounts allow you to invest in stocks, bonds, ETFs, or mutual funds, giving you the flexibility to grow your wealth without the restrictions of a TFSA.

The catch? Unlike TFSAs and RRSPs, you'll pay taxes on the profits (capital gains) only when you sell your stocks and lock in those capital gains. This means any money you make from cashing out investments is subject to taxation. So, it's important to plan your moves strategically based on your tax situation to keep more of your profit.

D. FHSA

The FHSA, introduced in 2023, is a big deal for those aiming to buy their first home. It combines the best of both worlds by offering tax-free growth on your investments, much like a TFSA, while scoring a tax break on what you put in, like an RRSP. That combo makes it a powerful tool for anyone saving up for their first home, helping you save effectively for a down payment. Even better, when you use the funds for your first home, both the contributions and the earnings are tax-free, making it a fantastic way to stretch your savings as far as they'll go.

This type of investment is also subject to rapid fluctuations; therefore, multiple factors must be considered before you begin investing with FHSA.

Make Your Tools Work for You

Once you've chosen the right accounts, put them to work. Spread your money across different types of investments to reduce risk, ensuring each account serves a purpose in your long-term strategy. Stay on top of matters, just like any job needs regular check-ins; your investment does too. Setting up your financial command centre isn't just about choosing accounts; it's about being prepared for anything.

A goal without a plan is just a wish.

ANTOINE DE SAINT-EXUPÉRY

MAKING THE FIRST MOVE:
OPEN AN INVESTMENT ACCOUNT

Establish your financial command posts (setting up your accounts) to deploy your capital. The first move in any operation is critical. It's the decision to advance and kick things off right. The same holds true for your financial path. Opening investment accounts is the first decisive action that gets the ball rolling. Laying down your financial foundation is the moment when you steer your money and make it count.

Let me share something from my own experience. For years, I kept meaning to open my investment accounts. I'd get all fired up about it, make a mental note, and then, nothing. It was like "soon" but never now. Never quite close enough to tackle. I procrastinated hardcore. I would sit there, researching all these accounts, only to bounce to something else to do. Every time, it was a deep inner debate: "Maybe tomorrow or next week," you know, the classic "I'll do it later" trap we all fall into.

But when I finally pulled the trigger and opened the accounts, everything changed. Suddenly, it was like I had unlocked a new level in the game of life. The clouds parted, the sun shone down, and I could hear opportunity knocking. No more hesitation. No more excuses. Looking back, I am kicking myself: "Seriously? I dragged my feet on this for years?" So much time was wasted, and I could have been growing my money, but it was gone. Most people hesitate and wait for the "perfect time." But here's the kicker: there's no such thing. The perfect time is always right now. Take that first swing; everything else will fall into place. It's like setting up your own financial battlefield, except this time, you're winning the war. The only thing holding you back is your own hesitation. The terrain will be clearer once you take that first step into the fog.

Choosing Your Financial Command Posts

To begin building wealth, you need the right accounts that have been previously examined. Each is designed to serve a unique purpose, just as each military unit plays a different role in a mission. Here's how to start:

Step 1: Choose a Financial Institution

Once you've decided which account suits your goals, it's time to select a financial institution to open your account. Whether you prefer a traditional bank or an online brokerage platform, make sure they offer the account types you want and have low fees, easy access to your investments, and good customer support. For example, if you're frequently on the move or deployed, an online brokerage with a robust mobile app can keep everything simple wherever you are. Me? I choose my bank and the platforms they offer. It has low fees, and some don't charge any commissions at all. More on my own account picks later.

Step 2: Complete The Application Process

Opening an investment account usually means filling out an application and providing your name, address, social insurance number (SIN), employment info, and a bit of ID proof. They'll likely want something like a driver's licence or any sort of documentation to confirm who you are.

Truthfully, filling out forms is about as exciting as cleaning your dirty weapon. It's the desk job version of a tactical retreat. Picture a twenty-kilometre ruck march with a heavy pack; it's not a blast while you are at it, but you'll feel like a champion once it's behind you. Sure, it's not as thrilling as the admin stuff you knock out before a big relocation to your desired posting, like an OUTCAN, but get it done. Once you've completed it, the real joyride begins.

Step 3: Fund the Account

With your account ready, it's time to deposit money. For a TFSA or RRSP, you can start with a lump sum or set up automatic contributions from your pay (ensure that you don't go over your contribution limits). For CAF members, setting up automatic deductions from your monthly pay can ensure you stay on track without thinking about it. Even small, regular deposits will add up over time and put your wealth-building strategy into motion faster than reloading your mags with ammo. Then the real fun begins: watching your fund grow and work for you.

Step 4: Begin Investing

Now that your account has some ammo in it, it's time to put your money to work, like deploying your troops into the field. This is where your investment strategy steps up. If you're just starting up, ease into it like a recruit fresh out of basic. You might consider low-risk investments like index funds or ETFs. Solid, reliable choices that give you a foothold without jumping into the deep end.

Once you've got your boots muddy and bearings straight, you can manoeuvre into sharper territory and branch out to individual stocks or bonds. The idea is simple: start small, spread your forces to outflank risk, and dig in for a long campaign. Just like in any military operation, pacing yourself ensures you don't burn out early. Start slow and gradually increase your exposure as you gain experience. Don't feel pressured to follow someone else's timeline. What works for them may not fit your mission. Financial success is a marathon, not a sprint. Stay focused on your goals, adapt when necessary, and let your plan evolve as your comfort with investing grows.

Step 5: Monitor and Adjust

Just like a military operation, staying flexible and adjusting as needed is key. Regularly review your accounts, track performance, and tweak your investments based on your goals, risk tolerance, and market conditions. For military members, being proactive is crucial, especially with frequent relocations or changing income. Start small but stay consistent. Contribute to a TFSA or RRSP every month. Over time, those small contributions compound, and with the right strategy, your wealth will mature and grow as you grow.

ASSET ALLOCATION: DEPLOYING YOUR RESOURCES

Investing isn't just about throwing all your resources into one area and hoping for the best. It's about strategic allocation, deploying your troops, equipment, and firepower across multiple fronts to maximize impact and minimize risk. The same principle applies when it comes to allocating funds. Asset allocation is all about spreading your resources across different types of investments (stocks, bonds, real estate, etc.) to ensure maximum growth while managing risk. It's your financial version of setting up a well-coordinated multi-unit operation.

The Basics of Asset Allocation

When you start investing, the first question you'll face is how to allocate your funds. When setting up a defence perimeter, you don't want everything in one place. The goal is to diversify, so if one area gets hit, you don't lose everything. Here's my take on this:

Stocks

If you're younger, you have the powerful advantage of time. By investing in a growing company today, you could see substantial rewards over the next twenty-five years. Picture a company in its early stages, and over the next two decades, it transforms into a dominant player in its industry. You'll reap the benefits from the appreciation of stock prices as the company grows. Stocks are your frontline troops; aggressive, fast-moving, and capable of delivering high returns. However, they can also be volatile, with the potential for setbacks along the way. The key is to balance your stock investments according to your risk tolerance. If you're young or have plenty of time to recover from market fluctuations, a larger portion of your portfolio in stocks might be the right move. If you're nearing retirement or simply prefer a more relaxed approach to managing your investments, consider shifting away from individual stocks and allocating more to stable, income-generating assets (stable dividend returns, bonds). This can help reduce stress and provide more predictable returns, giving you peace of mind as you focus on enjoying the next chapter of your life.

Bonds

Bonds are your support units; stable, reliable, and less likely to go rogue. They generate steady income, and while they don't have the same explosive growth potential as stocks, they can provide much-needed stability to your portfolio. I tend to keep a small chunk of my assets in bonds because I like having that safety net. It's like having a well-armed backup squad during a mission. Not as flashy, but essential. The benefits of bonds become even more apparent as you approach retirement. With a reduced ability to recover from market downturns, having bonds in your portfolio can help preserve capital and generate consistent income. As you near the end of your working years, bonds can provide the stability needed to safeguard your wealth while still allowing you to earn reliable returns.

Real estate
Real estate is like your fortified base. It requires more up-front capital and maintenance, but it appreciates over time and provides a solid foundation. If you're a CAF member with frequent postings, owning property can be a solid strategy for long-term growth. Think of it like buying a bunker in a location you know will grow in value. Plus, if you're lucky, you'll have a place to crash while on leave or come back to later in your career. Another major benefit is passive income. Once you have tenants, your property can generate consistent rental income, giving you an additional cash flow that can supplement your earnings. This income can be especially valuable during retirement when you may not have a regular paycheque. Real estate becomes more than just an investment; it's a reliable source of financial support.

This covers the key investment sectors that are a great starting point and an efficient way to build wealth. Now, let's dive deeper, and I'll share my personal perspective on investing.

My Personal Asset Allocation

The Multi-Unit Approach
Let me be clear! I'm not the type of investor who dumps everything into high-risk stocks or tries to time the market like I'm defusing a bomb. I'm all about balance. My strategy is like a well-trained unit: aggressive troops (stocks, including dividend payers) lead the charge, steady backup (bonds and

index funds) holds the line, and a fortified base (real estate) ensures long-term growth. A few years ago, I decided to invest in a couple of index funds and ETFs. These are like the infantry of the investment world, diversified, low-cost, and designed for steady growth. But I didn't throw all my capital into them. I've previously invested in some real estate, picking up a property in a town where I knew there was consistent demand for housing. Sure, it's not a high-speed, high-reward operation, but it paid off steadily and provided a solid backup in case the markets took a downturn. I knew I had something set aside in case of an emergency, not only appreciating in time but also providing steady returns. No need to constantly watch it; just let it do its thing while I focus on being a soldier.

My Appreciation for Dividend Stocks
I've become a huge fan over the years of dividend stocks. These aren't the flashy, high-risk rewards you see in the latest financial headlines. Oh no. These are the reliable, no-nonsense soldiers who show up every month, do their job, and leave you with something solid in return. They're my financial "field operators": consistent, dependable, and always on time to feed me regular intel. I want to make sure you fully grasp why I think they're such a powerhouse for building wealth. They're straightforward, reliable, and honestly, one of the best strategies out there. It worked for me and might just work for you. No need to overcomplicate it; dividend stocks are as practical as they get! Not rocket science.

The Silent Power of Long-Term Growth
Owning shares in companies like Coca-Cola or TELUS means regular dividend payouts, like a well-planned resupply drop. No surprises, just steady income. So, how do I pick them? Here are my strategy checks:

✓ **Track Record**—I look for companies with years of consistent payouts, like Canadian banks (Royal Bank, Enbridge, Bell). They're like seasoned veterans: stable, reliable, and battle tested.

✓ **Dividend Growth**—I prioritize stocks that increase payouts over time, not just high yields. Fortis, for instance, has raised its dividend annually for over forty years. That's the kind of stability I appreciate.

✓ **Payout Ratios**—I aim for companies with a healthy payout ratio (50—60%). You don't want to overextend.

Dividend stocks are my financial platoon. They provide consistent income, like a steady stream of rations to my portfolio. During market downturns, when growth stocks struggle, these companies keep delivering. They're the backbone of my strategy, offering stability and compounding returns. It's like having a squad of seasoned veterans who keep the mission on track, even when the battlefield gets chaotic. Companies with a strong history of paying dividends, often referred to as "Dividend Aristocrats," are like the decorated officers of the financial world. They've proven their ability to perform under pressure and reward their shareholders year after year.

My approach is simple—balance. However, I allocate a big portion of my portfolio to dividend stocks for steady income while leaving room for growth opportunities. It's not about chasing the next big thing, but rather about building a resilient, well-rounded portfolio that can weather any storm. When picking dividend stocks, I keep it straightforward and focus on:

- Reliable companies with a history of consistent payouts.
- Prioritize dividend growth and stability.

- Reinvest dividends to let compounding work its magic.
- Diversify across sectors to protect against volatility.

It's a slow and steady approach and nothing flashy, just a disciplined, long-term game plan. Dividends are my MVP, supplying passive income that compounds over time. Constant accumulation leads to significant returns.

So, what are you waiting for, soldier?

Here's a list of some major Canadian banks that pay dividends, along with their current approximate dividend yields:

- Royal Bank of Canada (RY)
- Toronto-Dominion Bank (TD)
- Bank of Nova Scotia (BNS)
- Bank of Montreal (BMO)
- National Bank (NA)

Canada's largest banks have a long history of stable dividend payments. They're a great starting point for building a dividend-focused portfolio.

CANADIAN BANKS			
BANK	**YIELD / YEAR**	**INVESTMENT**	**YEARLY DIVIDEND**
RY	3.40%	$10,000	$340
TD	5.05%	$10,000	$505
BNS	5.76%	$10,000	$576
BMO	4.44%	$10,000	$444
CM	4.28%	$10,000	$428
NA	4.20%	$10,000	$420

Data as of January 1, 2025

Various rockstar companies have been dropping steady dividend payouts and consistently delivering over the years. They're also a great starting point for building a dividend-focused portfolio. Here's a list of a few good long-term companies to consider for their dividends:

- Telus Communications (T)
- Manulife (MFC)
- Enbridge (ENB)
- Bell Communications (BCE)

CANADIAN COMPANIES AND DIVIDENDS					
COMPANY	YIELD / YEAR	STOCK PRICE	SHARES	INVESTMENT	YEARLY DIVIDEND
T	8.17%	$21.08	6,640	$140,000	$11,425
MFC	3.74%	$29.91	1,672	$50,000	$1,872
ENB	5.96%	$43.24	1,156	$50,000	$2,982
BCE	12.32%	$34.61	2,888	$100,000	$12,301
				Yearly Return	≈$28,580

Data as of January 31, 2025

Several top US companies have consistently paid steady dividends over the years, making them solid picks for building a dividend-focused portfolio. Here are a few worth considering:

- Altria Group Inc (MO)
- Exxon Mobil Corp (XOM)
- 3M Company (MMM)
- Coca-Cola Company (KO)

AMERICAN COMPANIES AND DIVIDENDS					
COMPANY	YIELD / YEAR	STOCK PRICE	SHARES	INVESTMENT	YEARLY DIVIDEND
MO	6.93%	$52.23	400	$20,892	$1,447.80
XOM	3.65%	$106.54	100	$10,654	$389.89
MMM	1.94%	$149.63	100	$14,963	$290.29
KO	2.95%	$63.48	100	$6,348	$187.27
				Yearly Return	≈$2,315.25

Data as of January 31, 2025
Note: Keep in mind that yields can fluctuate based on changes in stock prices and dividend payouts, so it's a good idea to verify the latest data before making any investment decisions.

Building Wealth with Residential Income

Let's talk about real estate, not just as a place to live, but as a powerhouse (pun intended) to build wealth. So, you buy a home in Petawawa during your first military posting. Fast-forward four years, and you're posted to Cold Lake. Instead of selling, you rent out your Petawawa home. Over time, that property provides a steady income stream. By the time you retire, you could own multiple properties across Canada, each one padding your financial stability.

The Landlord

Take my friend Gary (well, retired military), for example. He bought a duplex near the Military Base in Petawawa, lived in one unit, and rented out the other. The rental income covered his mortgage, and he even had extra cash flow each month. Over time, the property's value doubled, and Gary used the equity to move into his dream home while keeping the duplex as a rental. But Gary didn't stop there. He leveraged his success to buy three more properties, all rented to reliable tenants. Because he was so close to the base, finding renters was easy. Military personnel and their families were always looking for housing.

Today, Gary's real estate portfolio is a money-making machine, generating passive income while he enjoys retirement with his wife, Lianne, in their dream chalet.

Gary's story is a prime example of how real estate can transform your wealth-building journey. It's not just about buying a home; it's about creating a strategic asset that works for you, grows in value, and opens doors to new opportunities. Whether you're near a base or in a growing community, real estate can be your path to financial freedom in ways you might not expect.

Of course, owning real estate, whether for personal use or income, comes with responsibilities and risks. Think maintenance costs, property taxes, and the occasional market dip. Before making any big commitment it's important to carefully assess your financial situation and long-term goals and whether owning real estate is the right avenue for you.

Acquiring Real Estate

There's no shortcut here. Unless you inherit a large sum or have generous parents willing to lend you money, you'll need patience to save for a down payment and other home-buying costs. This could take months or years, depending on your finances. A simple way to start? Set money aside. For Canadians, there's a smart new option to save while getting tax breaks: the FHSA.

First Home Savings Account

Introduced in January 2023, the FHSA is a game-changer for Canadians looking to buy their first home. It combines the best of both worlds: contributions are tax-deductible (like an RRSP), and the money grows tax-free (like a TFSA).

With housing prices through the roof, saving for a 20% down payment can feel impossible nowadays, especially for military families juggling rising costs. An FHSA allows your savings to grow tax-free until you're ready to buy your future home. It's a smart way to build your down payment while waiting for the perfect time to make your move. Unused contributions carry forward, and you can invest the funds in stocks or other products to grow your savings.

But here's the catch—investing comes with risks. Market volatility could shrink your savings, so it's smart to consult a financial expert to understand your risk tolerance and choose the right investment strategy with this type of account. To qualify for tax-free withdrawals, you must be a first-time homebuyer. If you've owned a home before, you'll need to wait at least five years after selling to qualify.

Decisive factor? If you're thinking about buying a home, opening an FHSA and starting to contribute could be a smart move. It's one of the most effective ways to save, especially in today's challenging market.

FHSA CONTRIBUTION LIMITS		
YEAR	ANNUAL LIMIT	TOTAL LIMIT
2023	$8,000	$8,000
2024	$8,000	$16,000
2025	$8,000	$24,000
2026	$8,000	$32,000
2027	$8,000	$40,000

If you contribute $3,000 in 2023, you can carry over the unused $5,000 to future years provided you stay within the total contribution limits. By 2025, you can contribute up to $24,000, and by 2027, the maximum is $40,000.

Like a TFSA, you can invest your FHSA funds in the stock market or other options, but keep in mind that market volatility could reduce your available cash at withdrawal. It's wise to consult a financial expert to guide your investment choices based on your risk tolerance and timeline. To make tax-free withdrawals, you must be a first-time homebuyer. If you've never owned a home, you're automatically eligible; if you've previously owned one, you must wait five years before qualifying again. If you own a rental property and have never lived in it, you can be eligible for an FHSA.

What's the Minimum Holding Period for an FHSA?

None. You can withdraw funds at any time, as long as it's a qualifying withdrawal for a first home purchase. If you're planning to buy a home soon, the FHSA offers a powerful short-term tax advantage:

- It reduces your taxable income for the year.

- The contribution creates a tax deduction, which may lead to a tax refund.

- The withdrawal is tax-free.

- The money you save on taxes can go toward your home purchase.

- You can maximize tax savings and use the funds right away.

Let's break this down further, assuming the following:

- Income: $100,000

- Contribution: $16,000 ($8,000 in 2023/$8,000 in 2024). Contributions must be made between January 1 and December 31 to qualify for a tax deduction in the following filing year.

- Adjusted taxable income: $100,000—$16,000 = $84,000

- Resident of Ontario

- No other deductions or credits

NO FHSA VS. FHSA CONTRIBUTION		
TAX (ONTARIO) FILING 2024–2025	**NO FHSA CONTRIBUTION (TAXABLE = $100,000)**	**WITH $16,000 FHSA CONTRIBUTION (TAXABLE = $84,000)**
Federal Tax: 15% on first $55,867	$8,380.05	$8,380.05
Federal Tax: 20.5% on amount above $55,867	$9,053.17 (on $44,133)	$5,776.27 (on $28,133)
Total Federal Tax	$17,433.22	$14,156.32
Ontario Tax: 5.05% on first $51,446	$2,598.02	$2,598.02
Ontario Tax: 9.15% on amount above $51,446	$4,441.60 (on $48,554)	$2,978.55 (on $32,554)
Total Ontario Tax	$7,039.62	$5,576.57
Total Tax Owing (Federal + Ontario)	$24,472.84	$19,732.89
Tax Savings from $16,000 FHSA Contribution	—	$4,739.95

Financial Outcome: $16,000 FHSA contribution:

- Your taxable income drops from $100,000 to $84,000.
- Your total tax owing drops by $4,739.95.
- If your employer withheld more than $19,732.89 in taxes, you may receive a refund.

A perfect example of this advantage is me and my wife's plan to relocate in 2027 or 2028, when housing prices—especially in Ontario—could be much higher. By contributing $40,000 to the FHSA then and withdrawing it immediately to buy our new home, we not only fund the purchase but also claim a $40,000 tax deduction for 2028. This could significantly lower our taxable income and potentially yield a tax return of over $11,000 based on my current income alone.

The FHSA allows tax-free withdrawals at any time, if qualifying conditions are met, making it one of the most powerful tools for first-time homebuyers in Canada.

By 2027, you could contribute up to $40,000, unlocking major savings and a potential massive tax return, while growing your home-buying fund. If homeownership is your goal, the FHSA offers a smart way to save and offset Canada's high housing costs. Open an FHSA and start contributing today to take advantage of its benefits.

Why Rental Properties

There are plenty of ways to grow your wealth, but one of the best ways to do so while earning passive income is through real estate, specifically rental properties. If you've got a chunk of money sitting in your bank account earning next to nothing (think 0.05% interest), you're missing out on a big opportunity. That $50,000 you saved up from your last tour is just sitting there, not working for you at all. Leaving it in your bank means you're not only earning nothing, but inflation is also silently eroding your money's value. Right now, inflation in Canada is running higher than usual, over 5% as of January 2023. That means if you had $100,000 last year, it's worth less than $95,000 this year, and even less as time goes on. Inflation is like a hidden enemy attacking your savings, year after year.

So, instead of letting your money lose value, why not invest in a rental property? Sure, you'll no longer have that $100,000 sitting in your bank, but now you'll have a property generating passive income and growing your overall wealth. It's a way to combat inflation and increase your cash flow at the same time.

Before jumping into real estate, I recommend speaking with experts in both finance and real estate. They can help you navigate the process, from taxes to mortgage rates to choosing the right property. Everyone's situation is different; things like your credit score, down payment, and borrowing power will all come into play. So, get the advice you need to make the best decision for you.

Six Unit Multiplex

- **Cost**: $550,000 (2021)
- **Deposit**: 25% or $137,500
- **Mortgage Rate**: 2.34%
- **Mortgage Payment**: $2,600 per month

RENTAL INCOME		
PROPERTY UNITS	YEAR 2021	YEAR 2024
UNIT 1	$850	$1,200
UNIT 2	$900	$1,100
UNIT 3	$1,000	$1,400
UNIT 4	$950	$1,500
UNIT 5	$750	$1,200
UNIT 6	$750	$1,400
TOTAL REVENUE	$64,400	$93,600

This example can be applied to other rental property genres. It makes absolute sense to invest in rental properties if your goal is to create another stream of income. This type of investment will secure you for the long term and continue to generate income even long after you are gone. This type of asset can also be passed down to future generations and provide for your family for many years. Buy assets that will fund your retired lifestyle with passive income.

In Canada, rental income is fully taxable, and every dollar must be reported on your tax return. It gets added to your overall income, which could bring you into a higher tax bracket if your rental cash flow is strong. Another downside is that you won't receive a principal residence exemption upon the sale of your rental property. However, only 50% of the profit is taxable. In comparison to your main residence, upon selling, you can keep 100% of the profit.

CRA TAX BRACKET CALCULATION		
NEW TAXABLE INCOME AS OF 2025		
	Year 2025	Tax Rates
CAF (SGT. PAY)	$88,560	20.5%
RENTAL UNIT	$93,600	
TOTAL REVENUE	$182,160	29%

From this example above, you jump from a 15% tax rate to a 29% tax rate for the year 2025. Something to fully consider when your income increases and how each bracket applies to your level of income. Now, that doesn't mean that your overall income will be taxed at 29%. In Canada we have a Progressive Tax System, where each bracket will be taxed accordingly. Provincial brackets apply too.

PROGRESSIVE TAX SYSTEM		

FEDERAL INCOME TAX RATES FOR 2025

CRA TAX BRACKETS	YEAR 2025	TAX RATES
1	$57,375 or less	15%
2	$57,375.01 to $114,750	20.5%
3	$114,750 to $177,882	26%
4	$177,882.01 to $253,414	29%
5	Over $253,414	33%

PROVINCIAL INCOME TAX RATES FOR 2025		

ONTARIO

CRA TAX BRACKETS	YEAR 2025	TAX RATES
1	$52,886 or less	5.05%
2	$52,886.01 to $105,775	9.15%
3	$105,775 to $150,000	11.16%
4	$$150,000 to $220,000	12.16%
5	Over $220,000	13.16%

Tax rates by province or territory, based
on residency on December 31 of each year.

Before investing in rental properties for passive income, thoroughly understand the associated risks and challenges. This knowledge will help you fully leverage available tax credits and deductions to optimize your capital gains.

Real Estate Alternative

If managing a rental property doesn't appeal to you, then owning a Real Estate Investment Trust (REIT) can be a great alternative to owning rental properties, as previously introduced. By owning shares in REITs, investors gain exposure to a variety of properties and property types. Rather than being limited to just one or a few rental properties, investors will be exposed to a wider range of properties, such as commercial properties that include shopping centres, office buildings and more, which may not be accessible to individual investors with less money. REITs will provide you with passive income through dividends, as REITs are required by law to distribute more than 90% of their earnings to shareholders.

This can be beneficial for CAF members who are seeking a regular stream of income from their investments. A big majority of REITs pay their dividends monthly, just like you would get rent from a tenant if you owned an apartment building or any other rental property.

Lastly, if one day you don't want to hold the REIT anymore, you can sell it on the stock market. Unlike a physical residence, where you will have to go through legal and administrative procedures, REITs make it easier for investors to rid themselves of those obligations.

- **FCR.UN**: First Capital REIT
- **KMP.UN**: Killam Apt REIT

CANADIAN REIT			
COMPANY	**YIELD / YEAR**	**SHARES**	**YEARLY DIVIDEND**
FCR	5.34%	2,000	$1,780
KMP	4.33%	4,000	$2,880
		Yearly Return	$4,660

Data as of January 1, 2025

Residential Empire

My in-laws own a few properties, and my father-in-law han-
dles the residential income himself. Once everything's set
up with good tenants, it's pretty low maintenance. Just collect rent each month and let the property do its thing. It's
like earning dividends, but with a bit more effort upfront.
Of course, there are challenges, like tenants falling behind
on payments, but that's part of the game. The good news
is, even when they're late, they usually catch up, and if not,
there are legal options to take care of it.

It's really that simple. You don't need to overcomplicate
things unless something comes up that needs attention. My
father-in-law was the one who first got me into real estate
investing and showed me the ropes. He taught me all the ins
and outs of the business, and I quickly saw the huge potential. I didn't think twice about jumping in and teaming up
with him on his venture.

Learning from someone with experience has been invaluable, and I've gained so much over the years. Honestly, I
sometimes wish I'd met my wife sooner just for that reason. Her family owns a few properties that bring in steady
monthly income. Not only has it helped grow their wealth,
but it's also provided extra cash flow to cover everyday

expenses like bills, travel, and car payments. It has also opened even more opportunities to invest and grow the family income.

Incorporating Your Rental Properties

Thanks to my father-in-law's advice, my wife and I have grown our wealth, in part, through real estate strategy. One powerful strategy we use is incorporating assets like rental properties into a company or family trust, which helps separate business income from personal income. This keeps your salary unaffected and your business finances independent. The biggest perk is asset protection. If something goes wrong, incorporating shields your personal assets from creditors. It's a safety net for your finances. For tax benefits, it's best to consult with an accountant to ensure you're minimizing taxes effectively. A financial adviser can also help you map out the best approach for your situation. For now, it's something to keep in the back of your mind.

Rich Father Poor Father

My story takes me back to a book I read years ago: *Rich Dad Poor Dad* by Robert Kiyosaki. If you haven't read it yet, I highly recommend diving into it. It truly changed my view on money and investing. My biological dad reminds me a lot of Kiyosaki's "poor dad," a smart, hardworking guy who played it safe and focused on saving. He had a steady job and was well-respected, but investing wasn't part of his world. I understand why. He was the first in his family to come to Canada and arrived with very little. He had to build everything from scratch, facing challenges most Canadians don't experience. For him, the goal was always to work hard and save enough to get by. That's something many immigrants experience, and it's hard to fully grasp unless you've lived through it.

On the other hand, I had my father-in-law. He had a stable government job, made good money, and contributed to a pension fund for a comfortable retirement. But he wasn't afraid to take risks. He ventured into a few businesses, some of which didn't work out, but he learned valuable lessons along the way. Today, he owns multiple rental properties in Montreal. When he started, real estate was much cheaper, and those who invested back then are now sitting pretty with a net worth well over a million dollars.

By any measure, my father-in-law is wealthy. It's not just about his impressive real estate portfolio, his paid-off cars, or his long list of travels. What really stands out is that he created multiple streams of income through his properties. Plus, the solid pension from his government job adds to his financial security. He's set up for a comfortable retirement, no doubt about it.

My allocation is tailored to my goals, risk tolerance, and timeline, but it may not suit everyone. For me, a mix of dividend stocks, index funds, and stable income-generating assets works best, offering growth, stability, and peace of mind.

ESTABLISHING A TACTICAL TIMELINE: THE FINANCIAL CAMPAIGN

Establish specific goals and timelines for every investment. For every financial campaign, your timeline acts as a strategic plan, guiding how you allocate your capital and decide when to adjust your approach. It should align with your unique financial objectives and family situation, but keep in mind that patience is key. Extended periods of investment often lead to greater returns. The duration you commit to will influence the overall outcome, just like a carefully executed operation where timing and persistence are critical to successful missions.

Short-Term

For short-term investments, the goal might be to earn quicker returns, but it comes with higher risk. These investments require constant monitoring and a good understanding of market fluctuations. The risk of needing the money in a short timeframe can put you into situations where you're forced to liquidate your investments at a loss. This is why it's crucial to only invest money you don't need in the immediate future. If you think you'll need it for a house down payment, an emergency fund, or something similar in a year or two, don't tie it up in stocks or high-risk assets. If you have to withdraw the cash too soon, your investment value may have dropped and you may need more time to recover.

Long-Term

On the other hand, long-term investments, like dividend stocks and rental properties, are like setting up a base that you plan to hold for years. When you give your investments time to grow, the compound effect takes over. By holding onto solid dividend-paying stocks and rental properties, you're not just relying on stock price increases; you're also collecting regular payouts, which you can reinvest to buy even more shares. Over time, this creates a snowball effect, where your dividend income grows larger, providing you with passive income well into your later years, especially after active duty.

	DIVIDENDS PORTFOLIO				
TICKER SYMBOL	ANNUAL YIELD	TOTAL INVESTMENT	AVERAGE COST	SHARES HOLD	DIVIDEND PAYOUT
T.TO	8.17%	$96,000	$24	4,000	$7,843.2
BCE	12.21%	$64,500	$43	1,500	$7,875.45
ENB	6.16%	$44,000	$44	1,000	$2,710.4
BIR	6.67%	$20,000	$8	2,500	$1,334
LIF.TO	10.18%	$29,000	$29	1,000	$2,952.2
MFC	3.72%	$30,000	$25	1,200	$1,116
	Total	$283,500		Total	$23,831.25

As of January 2025. Annual yield may vary from the time of writing.

- **Annual Dividend Income**: $23,831.25
- **Quarterly Payout (every 3 months)**: $5,957.81

Based on the portfolio above, by investing $283,500 in dividend stocks, you're receiving passive income of $23,831.25 a year, or $5,957.81 every three months.

When starting with dividend stocks, don't expect overnight wealth unless you've got a money tree! Early returns may be small, and sometimes as little as $20, but with time, those small gains will grow into much larger amounts. It's like planting a seed that eventually becomes a money tree (without the watering).

Patience and discipline are key. The longer you stay invested, the more your money works for you. Dividend stocks can be a powerful way to build wealth and create passive income that can supplement your earnings, especially as you transition out of active service. Stick with it, and the results will pay off.

The Rule of 72

Now, this may be unfamiliar to a lot of folks, but this is a simple way to figure out how long it will take for your investment to double based on a certain rate of return. You take the number 72 and divide it by your annual rate of return (expressed as a percentage/yield). The result gives you the number of years it will take for your money to double. Alright, let's refine that a bit with some added clarity!

The Rule of 72 helps you estimate how long it'll take for your investment to double, but it's important to remember that this is based on one key factor: reinvesting your dividends. This means you take the dividends you earn and put them back into buying more shares of the stock. By doing this, you take advantage of compounding. Your money is working for you and growing itself. Let's walk through an example, assuming you're not adding any more money to the investment (no extra deposits):

Imagine you've invested in dividend stocks, like Enbridge Inc. (ENB), starting on January 1, 2025. To estimate how long it will take for your investment to double, we can use the Rule of 72. You divide 72 by the annual return rate (6% in this case): 72 ÷ 6 = 12 years.

So, your investment would double in approximately twelve years at a 6% annual return. This is a helpful way to get a rough idea of how long it will take for your money to grow without making additional deposits. However, if you start adding extra contributions, you're taking things to the next level. Your wealth can grow significantly faster. But with the Rule of 72, the real magic happens when you reinvest your earnings, letting your money compound and grow on its own. It's like putting your investments on autopilot for long-term success. Think of it like a military mission: your "resources" (dividends) keep getting re-supplied and multiplied, helping you build momentum over time without needing to do much extra work.

Alright, let's tie this all together. Now that we've broken down the Rule of 72 and how reinvesting dividends works, do you see what I mean by time is your greatest ally?

The more time you give your money to grow through compounding by reinvesting those dividends, the bigger your returns will be. It's not a quick fix, but like any good military operation, it's all about patience and letting things build steadily. You don't need to rush or constantly add more ammo (cash). Just keep the resources flowing, and over time you'll see that your returns double, then double again, all thanks to the power of time and patience.

Assume BCE 12% yield remains consistent. By the time you retire, a mere $30,000 turns into $480,000 without additional contributions (72 ÷ 12 = 6 years).

BELL CANADA ENTERPRISES (BCE.TO)				
YEAR 1	6	12	18	24
VALUE $30,000	$60,000	120,000	$234,000	$480,000

If the Bank of Nova Scotia (BNS.TO) remains steady near 6.22% yield per year. When applying the same formula, (72 ÷ 6.22 = 11.5 years).

BANK OF NOVA SCOTIA (BNS.TO)				
YEAR 1	11	22	33	44
VALUE $30,000	$60,000	120,000	$234,000	$480,000

So, yes, time is your ally. It's the silent partner that, if you let it, can turn a small effort into something massive. Give your investments time to work, and you'll reap the rewards, just like waiting for a well-executed plan to come to fruition.

Note: Even a solid company like BCE might lower its dividend for several reasons. Things like economic uncertainty, inflation, or global recession fears can all put pressure on their operations. Cutting the dividend can be a strategic move, helping the company manage costs, pay down debt, or invest in growth. It's not always a bad sign. Sometimes it's just a pause to keep things sustainable in the long run. While a full dividend cut is rare, most strong, cash-generating blue-chip companies like BCE do their best to keep rewarding shareholders and will continue to give payouts.

A good example: as of May 1, 2025, BCE reduced its annual dividend from \$3.99 per share to \$1.75 per share, likely to realign with current economic conditions and priorities.

MONITORING OPERATIONS: REGULAR REVIEW

Just like in military operations, staying proactive and adjusting your strategy is crucial to success. Regular portfolio reviews help ensure your investments remain aligned with your financial goals and can adapt to shifting market conditions. As CAF members, you know how quickly plans can change. The same applies to your financial strategy. At least quarterly, take a step back and evaluate your assets:

✓ Are they still performing? *Check!*

✓ Are your investments still supporting your long-term goals? *Check!*

✓ Do you need to reconfigure your account? *Check!*

If you're about to retire or nearing a major financial milestone, you might want to shift toward safer investments like bonds or dividend-paying stocks to preserve capital. However, if you're still a few years away from that goal, stocks may be the right choice to maximize growth. In the same way you adjust tactics during a mission, don't let your aircraft run on autopilot. Reallocate assets if necessary to stay on course toward your objectives. For CAF members, relocation can be a common trigger for rethinking residential income properties. Let's say you own a rental property near your current base, but a new posting takes you elsewhere. If selling the property becomes necessary, it's important to adjust your strategy accordingly. Whether you sell to free up capital for your next move or simply adjust your portfolio to accommodate the changes in your life, staying adaptable is key. Regular reviews ensure you stay ready for whatever comes next, keeping your financial mission on track, no matter the circumstance.

AFTER ACTION REPORT

- **Start the right investment account to support effective growth.** Whether you choose TFSA, RRSP, FHSA, or a Non-registered Account, this fundamental step ensures your resources are allocated strategically, laying the foundation for effective wealth-building management.

- **Allocate your assets for maximum growth.** Strategically allocate your funds across various assets (stocks, bonds, ETFS, real estate, etc.), based on your goals, risk tolerance, and time horizon. This will ensure diversification and optimize growth.

- **Counteract market conditions effectively.** By setting a clear timeline with specific investment goals, whether short-term or long-term, keeping a timeline will guide your decisions, help you track progress, and allow for adjustments as market conditions evolve.

- **Conduct regular reviews for maximum performance.** Consistently evaluate your investments and overall portfolio performance. This will ensure you stay on course, adapt to market shifts, and optimize returns.

Your habits will determine your future.

JACK CANFIELD
The Success Principles

CHAPTER 5

BATTLE DRILLS
TRAINING FOR
FINANCIAL
RESILIENCE

IN THIS CHAPTER, we'll explore strategies to enhance your financial position by identifying and addressing situations that hinder progress. We will also explore the root causes behind why so many CAF members neglect financial planning, and uncover actionable strategies to shift toward a proactive, empowered mindset for long-term fiscal well-being. It's essential to recognize that the advice provided here may not be applicable to everyone and can vary based on personal circumstances. The insights shared here are based on my own experiences and beliefs in wealth building, and they should not be taken as a one-size-fits-all solution. I encourage you to carefully evaluate and assess any financial strategies before adopting them. This chapter will focus on several key areas:

1 Strategic Approach: Breaking Personal Barriers
2 Neutralizing Threats: Eliminate Harmful Behaviour
3 Operation Efficiency: Stop the Financial Leak

4   The Defence: Defending Your Wealth
5   Mission Growth: Growing Financial Expertise
6   Missteps: Lessons from the Frontline

Acting on these fronts will put you in the tank driver's seat, ready to tackle challenges and secure your future beyond the barracks. *Buckle up, soldiers, and let's roll out full charged!*

STRATEGIC APPROACH:
BREAKING PERSONAL BARRIERS

Most people: *"I don't have any money to invest."*
Solution: Start budgeting, cut back and limit your expenses.

Most people: *"I don't know how to invest."*
Solution: Professional Adviser (SISIP), books, podcast, online course, investment platforms.

Most people: *"I don't have the time."*
Solution: Instead of wasting your time watching unproductive shows or mindlessly scrolling through social media, use that time to focus on improving your finances.

Making excuses will
only delay your future.

My wife loves unwinding by playing video games and diving into anime on her phone, and let's not get started with mindless shows on Netflix. It's her way of escaping the grind and recharging, something I totally get. We all need that downtime, especially after a long day of work. While she's farming virtual fields or exploring anime worlds, I make sure our real-world finances are on track. Don't get me wrong, she brings in a solid income for our household, so I'm not complaining at all! I just handle the money side of things so she can keep doing what she loves. *Teamwork, right?*

You see, distractions are everywhere. Whether it's video games, social media, or binge-watching shows, it's easy to lose focus on some of the things that really matter; your financial future perhaps. Staying on top of your finances is like maintaining your gear. Neglect it, and things fall apart fast; rust sets in, and suddenly you're getting lectured by your drill sergeant. But stay disciplined and focused, and you'll always be mission ready, both on and off the field.

The key is to maximize your productivity. Instead of spending hours on distractions, carve out time to review your budget, track your spending, or learn about investing. Even thirty minutes a week can make a huge difference. Remember, every small step you take today is a building block for your financial success tomorrow.

Reality check! Stepping out of your comfort zone can feel like jumping out of a plane without a parachute. It's scary, uncomfortable, and downright intimidating. Truth be told— *no great accomplishment was ever achieved by being idle.* Whether it's mastering a new skill on base or building wealth, growth only happens when you push past fear and act. For many in the military, investing can feel like uncharted territory. Here are some common reasons why service members hesitate to invest and how to overcome them:

The Lack of Knowledge

"I don't know enough about investing." Sound familiar? You're not alone. Many of us feel overwhelmed by terms like "stocks," "bonds," or "compound interest." But here's the thing—you don't need to be a financial expert to start. Like basic training, you start with the fundamentals. Use resources like SISIP financial advisers, books, or even podcasts during your commute. Knowledge is your first line of defence.

The Lack of Money

"I don't have enough capital to invest." I get it. When I was a young private, I thought investing was only for officers with big paycheques. But here's the reality—it's not about how much you start with; it's about starting. Even $50 a month can grow over time. Cut back on non-essentials (like that extra streaming service or daily coffee run) and redirect those funds toward your future. Small steps lead to big wins.

The Lack of Time

"I don't have time to manage my money." Between deployments, training, and family life, time is precious. But here's the deal—you make time for what matters. Instead of scrolling through social media or watching shows on Netflix five hours a day, dedicate thirty minutes a week to your finances. Treat it like a mission briefing: short, focused, and actionable. Remember, consistency beats perfection.

The Fear of Risk

"What if I lose money?" This is a big one. The fear of losing hard-earned cash can paralyze even the bravest warriors among us. But here's a mindset shift—risky is having only one source of income. Diversifying your investments is like having multiple backup plans in the field. Start small, educate yourself, and build confidence over time. Every investor faces risks, but the real risk is doing nothing!

The Game Plan

To conquer these excuses, start with education. Learn about your options, whether it's TFSA, RRSP, ETFs, or real estate. Then, create a plan that aligns with your goals and risk tolerance. The sooner you start, the better. Time is your greatest ally, and procrastination is your enemy. Don't wait until you're older and responsibilities pile up. Start now, even if it's with small steps.

Move at Your Own Pace

Here's a hard truth: stop comparing yourself to others. You have no idea what someone else went through to achieve their current level of success. Maybe they started investing years ago or had a mentor guiding them. Instead of feeling discouraged, let their story inspire you. Learn from their wins and mistakes, but focus on your own journey. Your finances are your mission; treat them like your own enterprise. You don't have to be a financial genius to build wealth. With dedication, the right mindset, and consistent effort, you can achieve anything. Dedicate time each week to manage your finances, just like you'd maintain your gear or train for a mission. Your financial future is in your hands. Take charge, stay focused, and keep moving forward. Remember, your personal finance is your enterprise, and your enterprise is your life.

Finance, much like any mission, demands your time, effort, and unwavering commitment. It boils down to one simple thing—you are showing up, no excuses, no hesitation. Whether it's clear skies or a storm rolling in, you can't afford to be a fair-weather player. The real winners are the ones who continue to push forward, no matter the circumstances, when the rain is pouring or the sun is shining. Just like in military operations, success is built on relentless dedication, no matter the conditions. Show up, and the results will follow.

NEUTRALIZING THREATS:
ELIMINATE HARMFUL BEHAVIOUR

Harmful financial habits, like overspending, ignoring debt, or living beyond your means, can sabotage your wealth-building mission. A poorly planned operation, without discipline, results in mission failure. By identifying and fixing these behaviours early, you secure your financial basecamp and reduce stress. Less stress means you can serve with confidence and better support those who depend on you.

Don't Live Beyond Your Means

It's no secret that the more money you make, the more you tend to spend. When that promotion hits, it's tempting to celebrate. Maybe a round of drinks for the squad, a new car, or that ATV you've been eyeing for months. But here's the problem—lifestyle inflation can spiral out of control. Before you know it, you're draining your paycheque faster than you earn it.

Ask yourself—do I really need that seventy-inch TV, the latest iPhone, or a speedboat? Could I put that extra cash toward savings or investments instead? An increase in income doesn't mean you need to live excessively. In fact, it's the perfect opportunity to save more and invest wisely. If you spend every dollar you earn, you'll never get ahead. The key? Maintain or reduce your current expenses as your income grows. That's how you build and increase your wealth.

The Credit Card Traps

Credit cards can be your best ally or your worst enemy. Used wisely, they're a tool for building credit and managing cash flow. Used recklessly, they're a one-way ticket to debt. When your expenses exceed your income, credit card balances balloon, and your savings shrink. The result? Less money for investments, retirement, and emergencies. The solution? Spend less than you earn. Avoid the temptation to buy now and pay later. If you can't afford it today, you probably can't afford it tomorrow.

The E-Commerce Trap

We live in a world of instant gratification. With a few clicks, you can order anything from anywhere, often without leaving your couch. Apps and ads are designed to make spending effortless, feeding your brain with the latest trends and deals. But convenience comes at a cost—impulse buying. Here's the reality!

E-commerce has made it easier than ever to overspend. Packaging companies and delivery services are thriving, while your savings might not be. The solution? Exercise discipline. Before clicking BUY, ask yourself—do I really need this?

Do you know what I ask myself? How many shares of my favourite stock or company could I buy with this money instead? That's how deeply I'm committed to my finances.

The Power of Balance

It's not about cutting out all spending, it's about balance. Enjoy life, but don't let impulse buys derail your financial goals. If you've become addicted to online shopping, cut back on small things and track your spending. The goal? Leave more room for savings and investments.

Investing Starts Now, Not Later

One of my biggest regrets? Not investing sooner. I didn't come from a wealthy family, and financial education wasn't part of my upbringing. But here's what I've learned—the sooner you start, the better. Even small, consistent investments can grow significantly over time. Warren Buffett said it best: *"Investing is about time in the market, not timing the market."*

Don't wait for the "perfect" moment. Start now. Let compound interest and dividends work in your favour. Market timing is a rookie mistake. The stock market is unpredictable, influenced by global events, economic conditions, and more. Trying to buy low and sell high often leads to missed opportunities and unnecessary costs. Instead, focus on a long-term, diversified strategy. Stay invested, even during downturns. History shows the market eventually recovers.

S&P 500 CLOSE (USD) FROM 1990–2025

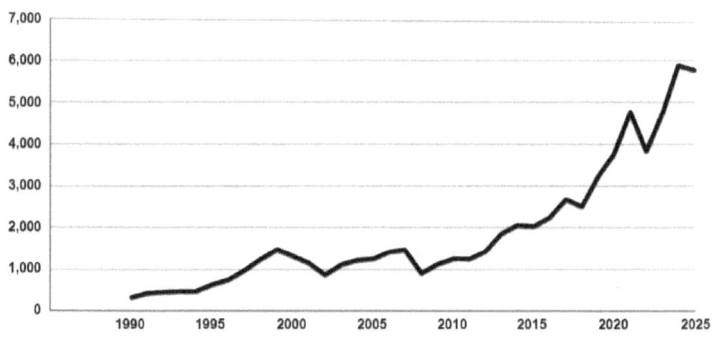

Data in (USD) at close for each year from 1990–2025

As a novice investor, I let emotions drive my decisions, and it cost me. I sold stocks during downturns, only to watch them rebound later. Now, I see market dips as opportunities to buy more at a discount. Remember what Mr. Buffett said: *"When others see fear, I see opportunity."*

When you're young, you have time to recover from mistakes. But that doesn't mean you should gamble with your money. A long-term strategy is your best bet for building wealth. The choice is yours—spend $150,000 today or invest it and potentially double your money in six or twelve years.

Let's imagine if I had applied today's investment knowledge twenty years ago when I joined the CAF. Suppose I'd invested my first $10,000 in McDonald's, our beloved fast food giant, back in January 2005, when shares were around $30. Today, with McDonald's stock trading over $280 or even more by the time I'm writing this, that initial investment could have grown over $200,000, not including dividends. A tasty reminder of the power of long-term investing.

STOCK PRICE APPRECIATION: MCDONALD'S (MCD)		
	2005	2025
PRICE PER SHARE	$32.10	$283.83
QUANTITY	1,000	1,000
MARKET VALUE	$32,100	$283,830

Data between Jan 31, 2005, and Jan 31, 2025

Selling your stocks at a loss is rarely a smart move unless you're in a situation where you urgently need cash. This comes down to effective financial management and planning. To avoid being forced into such a position, it's crucial to carefully allocate your funds and prioritize building an emergency reserve. By setting aside enough cash to cover unexpected expenses, you can avoid the need to liquidate your investments prematurely. Once you sell a stock at a loss, it's often difficult, if not impossible, to re-enter the market and repurchase the same stock at a lower price. This can lock in your losses and prevent you from benefiting from future growth.

Your financial mission is just as important as your military one. Eliminate harmful behaviours, stay disciplined, and focus on the long game. With patience and persistence, you'll secure your financial future and leave a legacy for those who depend on you.

OPERATION EFFICIENCY:
STOP THE FINANCIAL LEAK

Even the strongest vessel can sink if it's got a hidden leak. In this section, we're going to hunt down those sneaky financial leaks that are quietly draining your resources. These are the culprits I've seen time and time again:

- Adopting a pet
- Expensive addictions

And here's a simple but effective solution:

- Automating your savings

Adopting a Pet

Let's talk about one of the most common and often overlooked financial drains. I am not afraid to start with the toughest one—the cost of pet ownership. I'll use a dog as an example, but this logical process applies to any other animal companion as well, with some differences. Before I dive in, let me be clear—this isn't a call to abandon your furry friends. My goal is to educate, not criticize or push you in a certain way. I'm a dog lover myself and have owned two dogs in the past. One was a mixed poodle, and the other was a Yorkshire Terrier named Shoei (short for Chewbacca, thanks to his resemblance to a Star Wars character). Due to my military commitments, I had to rehome Shoei with my parents, who cared for him for over a decade before his passing. So, I understand the joy, the heartbreaks, and the challenges of pet ownership.

Pets are awesome; they're loyal, loving, and can be a great source of comfort, especially during deployments or stressful times. But let's be real—they're also expensive. Food, vet bills, grooming, toys, and unexpected medical emergencies can add up fast. It's like having a dependent who never grows up and never gets a job. If you're not careful, your furry friend can turn into a financial black hole. Before you adopt, make sure you've got a solid plan (and budget) to handle the various costs.

As many dog owners know, raising an animal requires a significant commitment of time and money. The specific needs of the animal, as well as its size, can greatly impact the level of effort and expense required. For those considering becoming a pet owner, it's important to thoroughly consider multiple factors before making the decision to adopt an animal. While owning a pet can be a fulfilling and rewarding experience for many individuals, it also comes with responsibilities that require significant time, effort, and resources. It's important to understand that pet ownership can have a tremendous impact on your lifestyle and finances.

The Not-So-Fun Factor of Pet Ownership

Owning a pet is a significant commitment, not just emotionally, but financially. According to the Ontario Veterinary Medical Association, the average annual cost of owning a dog in Canada is $3,724. That's over $300 a month! For military families, this can be a heavy burden, especially when duty calls and you need to arrange pet care during deployments or relocations.

Before you adopt, ask yourself these three questions:

- Can I afford this? Factor in food, vet bills, grooming, and emergency expenses.

- Do I have the time? Pets need exercise, socialization, and mental stimulation.

- What happens during deployments or moves? Who will care for your pet when you're away? This comes at a cost too.

Pets are a lifelong responsibility. If you're not prepared for the financial and time commitments, it's better to wait until your situation is more stable.

The Hidden Costs of Pet Ownership

Here's a breakdown of what you might spend annually on a dog:

- **Food**: $500—$1,000
- **Vet visits**: $500—$1,000 (more for emergencies)
- **Grooming**: $300—$600
- **Boarding**: $500—$1,000 (travel frequency depending)
- **Supplies**: $200—$400

These costs can strain your budget, especially if you're already juggling other financial priorities like saving for retirement or paying off debt.

The Various Treatments

- **Parasite Prevention**: $250—300
- **Exams & Vaccines**: $175—$200
- **Heartworm/Lyme test**: $100
- **Wellness Profile**: $135—$200
- **Fecal Exam**: $50—$90
- **Dental**: $600—$700
- **Total Cost**: $1,400—2,000 approximately

These numbers may vary depending on the service provided from local and provincial care providers.

My words to current pet owners. If you already have a pet, this isn't a call to rehome them. Instead, it's a reminder to plan. Set aside a pet emergency fund, budget for routine expenses, and explore pet insurance to mitigate unexpected costs. Your furry friend is part of the family, so make sure you're prepared to care for them, no matter what life throws your way.

For those considering a pet: if you're thinking about adopting, take a hard look at your finances and lifestyle first. Are you ready for the commitment? If not, consider volunteering at a shelter or fostering animals temporarily. It's a great way to enjoy the companionship of a pet without the long-term financial burden.

Thankfully, we have amazing friends who own dogs. I get to enjoy all the perks of spending time with their furry companions, playing, walking, and even taking care of them occasionally, without the long-term responsibility. I like to call it my "animal therapy moment." It's the perfect way to get my dose of dog love without the financial and time commitments that come with full-time pet ownership. We've also been incredibly fortunate to have friends who own horses too. Now, that's a whole different level of commitment. The costs involved add up to a significant sum, one I'm not ready to take on. But thanks to our generous friends, we've been able to experience the joy of these magnificent animals without the burden of ownership.

A huge shout-out to Sanda, Paul, Anne, Linda, James, and Leanne for sharing your animals with us. The memories we made at the ranch, riding, bonding, and simply being around those incredible creatures are priceless. We miss those days dearly and are so grateful for the joy you've brought into our lives.

Pets bring joy, companionship, and unconditional love, but they also come with a price tag. By understanding the costs and planning, you can ensure that pet ownership doesn't drain your resources or derail your financial goals. Remember, every dollar you save on unnecessary expenses is a dollar you can invest in your future.

Let's put the cost of owning a dog into perspective. The average annual cost of owning a dog in Canada is around $3,600. While the companionship of a pet is priceless, it's worth considering what that money could do if invested wisely.

	ADOPTING VS. INVESTING				
YEAR	YEARLY INVESTMENT	TOTAL INVESTMENT	YEARLY INTEREST	TOTAL INTEREST	TOTAL VALUE
1	$3,600	$3,600	$130.17	$130.17	$3,730.17
2	$3,600	$7,200	$428.58	$558.75	$7,758.75
3	$3,600	$10,800	$750.86	$1,309.61	$12,109.61
4	$3,600	$14,400	$1,098.94	$2,408.55	$16,808.55
5	$3,600	$18,000	$1,474.85	$3,883.40	$21,883.40
6	$3,600	$21,600	$1,880.83	$5,764.23	$27,364.23
7	$3,600	$25,200	$2,319.31	$8,083.54	$33,283.54
8	$3,600	$28,800	$2,792.85	$10,876.39	$39,676.39
9	$3,600	$32,400	$3,304.27	$14,580.66	$46,580.66
10	$3,600	$36,000	$3,856.62	$18,037.28	$54,037.28

This is an estimated cost of dog ownership, excluding inflation and the rise in prices

Numbers Don't Lie

The figures speak for themselves. Your monthly investment of $300.00 at an annualized interest rate of 8% could be worth over $50,000 after ten years when compounded yearly. That's money that could be reinvested into other income-generating assets, like real estate or dividend-paying stocks, creating even more financial opportunities.

Pets bring immense joy and companionship, and for many, they're worth every penny. However, it's important to recognize that not owning a pet can free up significant financial resources over your lifetime. It's a simple fact that for every dollar saved, there is a dollar that can be invested in your future of financial freedom. Whether you choose to own a pet or not, the key is to make informed decisions that align with your financial goals. If you're passionate about pets, plan ahead and budget for their care. If you're on the fence, consider the long-term financial impact and explore alternatives, like borrowing a friend's dog for occasional "animal therapy sessions."

At the end of the day, financial freedom is about making choices that empower you to live the life you want today and in the future.

Expensive Addictions

Cigarettes are one of the most expensive addictions out there. Simply put, it's wealth burned into fumes. How many of you started smoking during field exercises? Who can relate to that, eh? It's easy to fall into the habit, especially when you're out in the field, stressed, and looking for a way to unwind. But here's the reality—smoking doesn't just harm your health; it also drains your bank account. We all know the health risks: lung damage, increased risk of cancer, and a host of other issues. Doctors have been warning us for decades, yet many still struggle to quit. But have you ever stopped to think about the financial cost? Let's break it down.

The Financial Benefits of Quitting

Think about how many times you or your colleagues take those five-minute smoke breaks each day. If someone smokes ten cigarettes a day, that's nearly an hour of lost productivity. Now, I'm not here to argue whether non-smokers should get paid more (though that could be an interesting incentive for productivity!). Instead, let's focus on what you could gain by quitting.

I get it, quitting smoking isn't easy. But if the health warnings aren't enough to convince you, maybe the financial benefits will. Think about what you could do with that extra money: travel, invest, or simply enjoy more financial freedom. Whether it's smoking, unnecessary spending, or other financial drains, the key is to identify habits that hold you back and replace them with ones that move you forward. Every dollar saved is a dollar that can work for you, building a brighter, healthier, and wealthier future. So, what's it going to be, soldier? Will you let your habits control you, or will you take control of your habits? The choice is yours.

What if I told you that giving up cigarettes could save you thousands of dollars over your lifetime? *Let's do the math!*

The Cost of Smoking: Warrant Ash Puffalot's Story

Let's break down the financial hit of smoking using Warrant Puffalot as an example. The Warrant smokes about eight cigarettes a day, but for simplicity, let's round it to ten (half a pack). We'll leave weekends out of the equation. With the average pack of twenty cigarettes in Ontario costing $12.26, here's how Warrant Puffalot's habit stacks up:

TOBACCO EXPENDITURE			
TIMEFRAME	**CIGARETTES**	**PACKAGE**	**COST**
DAILY	10	1/2	$6.13
WEEKLY	70	3 1/2	$42.91
MONTHLY	280	14	$171.64
ANNUALLY	3,360	168	$2,059.68

That's $2,059.68 per year going up in smoke (another pun intended). And that's just for half a pack a day. If Warrant Puffalot smoked a full pack daily, the annual cost would double to $4,119.36.

What if Warrant Puffalot invested that money instead?

TOBACCO INVESTMENT FUND					
YEAR	YEARLY INVESTMENT	TOTAL INVESTMENT	YEARLY INTEREST	TOTAL INTEREST	TOTAL VALUE
1	$2,064	$2,064	$74.63	$74.63	$2,138.63
2	$2,064	$4,128	$245.72	$320.35	$4,448.35
3	$2,064	$6,192	$430.49	$750.84	$6,942.84
4	$2,064	$8,256	$630.06	$1,380.90	$9,636.90
5	$2,064	$10,320	$845.58	$2,226.48	$12,546.48
6	$2,064	$12,384	$1,078.35	$3,304.83	$15,688.83
7	$2,064	$14,448	$1,329.73	$4,634.56	$19,082.56
8	$2,064	$16,512	$1,601.23	$6,235.79	$22,747.79
9	$2,064	$18,576	$1,894.46	$8,130.25	$26,706.25
10	$2,064	$20,640	$2,211.12	$10,341.37	$30,981.37

Annual yield of 8% average

- **After 10 years**: Approximately $30,980
- **After 20 years**: Approximately $97,867
- **After 25 years**: Approximately $156,346

That's a substantial amount in potential savings at retirement, enough to fund a house, fund a comfortable retirement, or leave a legacy for loved ones. And that's just from quitting half a pack a day.

A mere $171.64 monthly in personal contributions can grow to $156,346 over your career, and that's without factoring in inflation or the rising cost of cigarettes, which will only increase your expenses year after year. By continuing to smoke, you're not just harming your health; you're burning through your wealth. Quit now, save thousands on insurance premiums as a non-smoker, and redirect that money toward building a secure financial future. The choice is clear—stop smoking and start investing.

For those who enjoy vaping, the financial impact is just as significant, if not more, as smoking, only with a bit more flavour. While the tempting tastes might make it seem harmless, vaping is far from healthy and comes with a hefty price tag too. A 30 ml bottle of vape juice can cost anywhere from $7 (lasting about five days with heavy use) to $50 for so-called "premium" brands. But let's be clear—there's nothing "premium" about sucking chemicals into your lungs.

What's worse, the endless variety of flavours can lead to impulse buying. Before you know it, you've built a collection of vape juices to match your mood or cravings, a habit that can easily cost more than traditional cigarettes. Don't let the sweet flavours cloud your judgment. Vaping isn't just harmful to your health; it's vaporizing your vault too.

Automating Your Savings

Automate and Accumulate

Like scheduling a consistent exercise routine, setting up automatic transfers from your chequing account to your savings or investment account can help improve your savings rate without requiring constant effort and attention. By automating money transfers, you can ensure that a portion of your earnings is set aside at a specific time and date, much like an automated exercise routine. You can't spend what you don't have. This system is beneficial for everyone and can help create a better savings rate.

By automating your savings, you don't have to remember to transfer money manually each time. It's convenient, and there is less of a risk that you will forget. By automating your savings, you also avoid procrastinating, which can help you reach your goals faster. It's like having an automatic reloading ammunition button. Compounding interest works very well over the long term. Missing a few saving opportunities can decrease your overall wealth if you miss too often.

In summary, avoid high-cost lifestyle choices like owning pets or falling into bad habits. Establish automatic transfers as your "financial standby orders" to stay consistently engaged. This is your personal commitment to "fall in" and set aside a specific amount each month, building a strong financial foundation. This is a commitment to yourself and your financial journey.

Shoot and Forget Wealth-Building Op

The CAF paycheque isn't just reliable, it's a force multiplier for wealth creation if used properly. Work with your Orderly Room (OR) to automatically divert a percentage of each pay directly to savings or investment accounts. This will set up a recurring operation for your finances. With zero-effort discipline, no manual transfers means no missed deposits. Even small contributions grow exponentially.

TACTICAL GROWTH RATE: NOVICE					
YEAR 10%	**DEPOSITS**	**INTEREST**	**TOTAL DEPOSITS**	**ACCRUED INTEREST**	**BALANCE**
0	$100.00	–	$100.00	–	$100.00
1	$1,200.00	$67.03	$1,300.00	$67.03	$1,367.03
5	$1,200.00	$687.05	$6,100.00	$1,808.24	$7,908.24
10	$1,200.00	$1,904.79	$12,100.00	$8,655.20	$20,755.20
15	$1,200.00	$3,908.33	$18,100.00	$23,792.43	$41,892.43
20	$1,200.00	$7,204.78	$24,100.00	$52,569.69	$76,669.69
25	$1,200.00	$12,628.47	$30,100.00	$103,789.03	$133,889.03
YEAR 8%	**DEPOSITS**	**INTEREST**	**TOTAL DEPOSITS**	**ACCRUED INTEREST**	**BALANCE**
0	$100.00	–	$100.00	–	$100.00
1	$1,200.00	$53.29	$1,300.00	$53.29	$1,353.29
5	$1,200.00	$524.11	$6,100.00	$1,396.67	$7,496.67
10	$1,200.00	$1,368.66	$12,100.00	$6,416.57	$18,516.57
15	$1,200.00	$2,626.91	$18,100.00	$16,834.51	$34,934.51
20	$1,200.00	$4,501.50	$24,100.00	$35,294.72	$59,394.72
25	$1,200.00	$7,294.36	$30,100.00	$65,736.66	$95,836.66
YEAR 5%	**DEPOSITS**	**INTEREST**	**TOTAL DEPOSITS**	**ACCRUED INTEREST**	**BALANCE**
0	$100.00	–	$100.00	–	$100.00
1	$1,200.00	$33.00	$1,300.00	$33.00	$1,333.00
5	$1,200.00	$305.37	$6,100.00	$828.94	$6,928.94
10	$1,200.00	$731.92	$12,100.00	$3,592.93	$15,692.93
15	$1,200.00	$1,279.35	$18,100.00	$8,840.26	$26,940.26
20	$1,200.00	$1,981.90	$24,100.00	$17,274.63	$41,374.63
25	$1,200.00	$2,883.52	$30,100.00	$29,799.10	$59,899.10

When your cash flow gets a promotion (deployment pay, rank bump, or finally crushing that motorcycle loan), deploy the surplus! Even a few hundred extra bucks monthly becomes a financial fireteam over time.

TACTICAL GROWTH RATE: INTERMEDIATE					
YEAR 10%	DEPOSITS	INTEREST	TOTAL DEPOSITS	ACCRUED INTEREST	BALANCE
0	$300.00	–	$300.00	–	$300.00
1	$3,600.00	$195.00	$3,900.00	$195.00	$4,095.00
5	$3,600.00	$1,956.26	$18,300.00	$5,168.85	$23,468.85
10	$3,600.00	$5,348.41	$36,300.00	$24,482.53	$60,782.53
15	$3,600.00	$10,811.51	$54,300.00	$66,576.57	$120,876.57
20	$3,600.00	$19,609.87	$72,300.00	$145,358.62	$217,658.62
25	$3,600.00	$33,779.74	$90,300.00	$283,227.09	$373,527.09
YEAR 8%	DEPOSITS	INTEREST	TOTAL DEPOSITS	ACCRUED INTEREST	BALANCE
0	$300.00	–	$300.00	–	$300.00
1	$3,600.00	$156.00	$3,900.00	$156.00	$4,056.00
5	$3,600.00	$1,510.00	$18,300.00	$4,034.95	$22,334.95
10	$3,600.00	$3,908.26	$36,300.00	$18,411.53	$54,711.53
15	$3,600.00	$7,432.10	$54,300.00	$47,983.34	$102,283.34
20	$3,600.00	$12,609.77	$72,300.00	$99,881.94	$172,181.94
25	$3,600.00	$20,217.47	$90,300.00	$184,585.91	$274,885.91
YEAR 5%	DEPOSITS	INTEREST	TOTAL DEPOSITS	ACCRUED INTEREST	BALANCE
0	$300.00	–	$300.00	–	$300.00
1	$3,600.00	$97.50	$3,900.00	$97.50	$3,997.50
5	$3,600.00	$894.33	$18,300.00	$2,431.02	$20,731.02
10	$3,600.00	$2,136.04	$36,300.00	$10,506.76	$46,806.76
15	$3,600.00	$3,720.80	$54,300.00	$25,786.74	$80,086.74
20	$3,600.00	$5,743.40	$72,300.00	$50,261.37	$122,561.37
25	$3,600.00	$8,324.81	$90,300.00	$86,470.95	$176,770.95

Now that you've secured your personal financial high ground, it's time to call in reinforcements. Imagine synchronizing your wealth-building offensive with your life partner. Two disciplined savers with a unified strategy. That's your

Special Forces of finance. You'll hit millionaire status faster than a CF-18 breaking the sound barrier. That's the power of combining interest both in your personal life and on the financial battlefield.

| | | | TACTICAL GROWTH RATE: ADVANCED | | |

YEAR 10%	DEPOSITS	INTEREST	TOTAL DEPOSITS	ACCRUED INTEREST	BALANCE
0	$1,000.00	–	$1,000.00	–	$1,000.00
1	$12,000.00	$670.28	$13,000.	$670.28	$13,670.28
5	$12,000.00	$6,870.54	$61,000.00	$18,082.38	$79,082.38
10	$12,000.00	$19,047.86	$121,000.00	$86,552.02	$207,552.02
15	$12,000.00	$39,083.32	$181,000.00	$237,924.27	$418,924,27
20	$12,000.00	$72,047.85	$241,000.00	$525,696.91	$766,696.91
25	$12,000.00	$126.284.67	$301,000.00	$1,037,890.35	$1,338,890.35

YEAR 8%	DEPOSITS	INTEREST	TOTAL DEPOSITS	ACCRUED INTEREST	BALANCE
0	$1,000.00	–	$1,000.00	–	$1,000.00
1	$12,000.00	$532.93	$13,000.00	$532.93	$13,532.93
5	$12,000.00	$5,241.12	$61,000.00	$13,966.70	$74,966.70
10	$12,000.00	$13,686.61	$121,000.00	$64,165.68	$185,165.68
15	$12,000.00	$26,269.09	$181,000.00	$168,345.14	$349,345.14
20	$12,000.00	$45,015.03	$241,000.00	$352,947.22	$593,947.22
25	$12,000.00	$72,943.60	$301,000.00	$657,366.57	$958,366.57

YEAR 5%	DEPOSITS	INTEREST	TOTAL DEPOSITS	ACCRUED INTEREST	BALANCE
0	$1,000.00	–	$1,000.00	–	$1,000.00
1	$12,000.00	$330.02	$13,000.00	$330.02	$13,330.02
5	$12,000.00	$3,053.66	$61,000.00	$8,289.44	$69,289.44
10	$12,000.00	$7,319.25	$121,000.00	$35,929.29	$156,929.29
15	$12,000.00	$12,793.52	$181,000.00	$88,402.65	$269,402.65
20	$12,000.00	$19,818.98	$241,000.00	$172,746.31	$413,746.31
25	$12,000.00	$28,835.17	$301,000.00	$297,991.00	$598,991.00

Call to Action? Report to your OR and request a "Voluntary Deduction." Designate targets like TFSA, RRSP, or savings account and execute them. Watch your wealth advance like a phase operation. You'll be unstoppable.

THE DEFENCE: DEFENDING YOUR WEALTH

Debt is one of the most formidable adversaries you'll face in the financial battlefield. Just as you would identify and neutralize threats in a combat scenario, you must confront debt head-on. High-interest liabilities like credit cards, car loans, or personal loans can act like a stealthy enemy, quietly eroding your wealth and derailing your financial mission if left unchecked. Treat it as a high-value target.

Debt Elimination

We've already covered why debt elimination is critical in a previous chapter. Now let's ensure you stay proactive. Here are my two battle-tested strategies to enforce resilience and keep you on track:

Two Tactical Methods

1 **Debt Snowball**—begin with the smallest debts. Pay them off first while keeping up with minimum payments on the rest. Each victory builds momentum, boosts morale, and keeps you driven to push forward.

2 **Debt Avalanche**—focus on high-interest debts first. This strategy cuts long-term costs and takes out the most dangerous threats early, ensuring you're fighting smarter, not harder.

Both methods demand discipline. Choose your tactic, the one that works for you, and execute it with precision. *Over!*

Eliminating debt neutralizes a major threat to financial freedom, freeing resources to invest, save, and amass wealth. Defeating debt is a critical mission to secure your financial future and achieve long-term success.

MISSION GROWTH: GROWING FINANCIAL EXPERTISE

Just like staying on top of your trade is key to advancing your career, levelling up your financial skills is mission-critical for your money game. Think of it like this—building wealth isn't a one-and-done deal; it's an ongoing operation that requires constant learning, adapting, and growing. Whether it's getting a grip on compound interest, making the most of tax-advantaged accounts, or nailing retirement strategies, expanding your financial know-how is how you hit your objectives. Train up, make smarter moves, and secure your financial future. *Roger that?*

Sharpen Your Skill

To dominate your financial journey, treat learning like your secret weapon. Dedicate time to devouring books, soaking up workshops, or absorbing wisdom from credible financial experts. Build a network of ambitious, like-minded go-getters. Wealth building thrives on shared momentum. I carve out time almost every day for financial learning and devour finance books over my weekends (shout-out to Peter Lynch, the author of *One Up on Wall Street*—this book boosted my knowledge on investing) and listen to financial podcasts while exercising. But the real magic? Surround yourself with individuals who get it. My buddy Raf, an avid investing nerd, introduced me to some trading skills and investing strategies over our lockdown during our career course in Winnipeg a few years ago. Now we swap stock tips daily like they're Netflix recommendations. Turns out, wealth building is way less lonely and way more fun when you've got a squad hyping you up.

Just as crucial is learning to spot and avoid common financial "Missteps." Impulse spending, poor budgeting, and neglecting emergency planning can easily derail your progress. So, stay disciplined and informed, you'll be ready to handle these setbacks and keep your financial mission on course.

Remember, growth doesn't happen overnight. Stay sharp, stay focused, and keep pushing forward. You're building a strong financial foundation, one step at a time. Copy that!

MISSTEPS: LESSONS FROM THE FRONTLINE

We're now treading into treacherous terrain. Ground where no prudent soldier should venture. I'll walk you through my own financial missteps to help you avoid making the same mistakes. Just as a single tactical error in combat can compromise an entire operation, one poor financial decision can create lasting setbacks.

I'll share my personal experiences, so you can learn from my errors. If you find yourself in a similar situation, consider this your call to action: retreat, regroup, and reassess your strategy before the problem escalates. This is you defusing a financial Improvised Explosive Device (IED). The sooner you address it, the less damage it will cause. Let's shine the light on ten common financial pitfalls I encountered, which you'll want to avoid:

1 Social validation
2 Appearances
3 Purchase of a brand-new car
4 Your social network
5 Your life alliance

6 Chasing the perfect time
7 FOMO
8 False authorities
9 Gambling
10 Not saving early on

I'll treat you like a new rookie from basic, *so listen up, recruit!* Learn from these missteps and you'll dodge debt-snipers, ambush impulse buys, and secure the high ground on Savings Hill. Avoid the traps that sabotage your wealth-building quest.

Social Validation

Spending money to show people how much money you have is the fastest way to have less money.

MORGAN HOUSEL,
The Psychology of Money

It's human nature to want to impress others with what we have, but this often leads us to buy things we don't need just to keep up appearances. I fell into this trap hard in my twenties. Why did I rent an apartment that swallowed 40% of my income? I wanted to impress my friends and family when they visited. Why did I buy a brand-new car at twenty-one with shaky financing? To turn heads on the street and impress dates. Why did I insist on paying for dinners I couldn't afford? So my friends would think I was doing well. But here's the truth—no one cared. My parents weren't dazzled by my fancy apartment, which had a "breathtaking" view of Montreal. They were more concerned about whether I was eating enough. And in three years, not one friend bothered to visit me there. My "generosity" at dinner? My friends were probably just thrilled to get a free meal, and most of the time, there were no returned favours. As for the strangers who saw me cruising in my new car or motorcycle, they didn't give a darn bullet. Think about it, when was the last time you were impressed by someone driving a flashy car? If you're like me, you were probably more annoyed by the noise they made passing by than anything else.

The reality is that spending money to impress others is a losing game. Nobody cares as much as you think they do, and you're left holding the bills, sometimes for years. If you're going to spend money, spend it on things that add real value to your life. Don't waste it trying to prove something to people who won't remember it tomorrow. Trying to keep up with others' lifestyles or spending to impress peers can lead to unnecessary debt. True wealth isn't about appearances, it's about financial security.

Appearances

What you wear is just a disguise, not the real story.

First impressions matter, especially in professional or social settings. How you present yourself influences how others perceive and interact with you, shaping personal and professional relationships. But appearances can be deceiving. Your neighbours might seem to have it all. Flashing the latest gadgets, wearing designer labels, and radiating confidence. But let's be honest; anyone with a credit card and the right attitude can *look* rich. That doesn't mean they *are* rich.

I used to buy expensive, branded clothes, convinced that people judged me by what I wore, whether walking down the street, sitting in a restaurant, or heading to school. But as I grew older, I realized how little that stuff matters. Now, I prioritize comfort. A pair of jeans I wear three times a week and a cozy sweater from four winters ago. As military members, you've got one less thing to worry about—what to wear every day. No need to stress over what to wear to work or waste money on new suits and shoes. It's efficient, practical, and lets you focus on what truly matters: being a soldier. Take a cue from the world's wealthiest—Mark Zuckerberg wears the same grey T-shirt in every interview. Steve Jobs (may he rest in peace) famously wore the same black turtleneck and jeans at every product launch. Warren Buffett, worth $90 billion, still drives his 1989 Volvo. These people didn't get rich by flaunting wealth; they focused on what truly matters—building wealth.

As the French proverb goes, *"L'habit ne fait pas le moine,"* the clothes don't make the monk. The goal isn't to *look* rich; it's to *be* rich. Fancy gadgets and designer labels won't build wealth; au contraire, they'll drain your bank account. If you don't have investments or a financial plan, you don't deserve that latest phone upgrade. Your old one works just fine.

Stop worrying about appearances. Focus on building real wealth, not the illusion of it.

Purchasing a Brand-New Car

Buying a new car to impress others
is like sending your money on a joyride;
it never stays long enough to pay off.

There are several reasons why buying a new car might not
be the best move:

- **Depreciation**—the moment you drive a new car off the lot,
  it loses value faster than a rookie loses their keys. In the
  first few months alone, its worth can drop by thousands.

- **High cost**—new cars come with hefty monthly payments,
  sky-high insurance, and a five to seven-year commitment.
  It's like having a mortgage on four wheels, except the car
  can't even pay for its own gas.

- **Interest rates**—financing a new car often means paying
  interest that inflates the total cost. It's like paying extra
  for a pizza and realizing you're stuck with pineapple on it
  for five years. (Sorry, Hawaiian pizza lovers, it's like kiwis
  on pizza for me!)

- **Maintenance costs**—new cars, especially luxury brands,
  can be high-maintenance. Repairs can cost more than a
  small vacation, leaving you with a savings account just
  for "Oops, my engine's broken" days.

- **Limited budget**—if you're already juggling debt and
  expenses, a new car stretches your finances thinner than
  a map in a soldier's pocket. It leaves little room for emergencies or long-term goals.

I drove my trusty Honda Civic for over fourteen years. Early on, the monthly payments were a constant reminder of my financial struggles, and it took five years to pay off. Even when the car was running strong, I resisted the urge to upgrade just to impress others. I knew my money was better spent elsewhere. It wasn't until I was in a stable financial position that I finally bought a new car: as a choice, not a necessity. If your current ride is reliable, hold off on the new-car itch. Save your money for things that appreciate, like your financial future.

Growing Your Network is Growing Your Net Worth

We are the average of the five
people we spend the most time with.

JIM ROHN

Our network of friends is often shaped by the circumstances we're born into, the neighbourhood we grew up in, the schools we attended, and the coworkers we interact with daily. These connections form the foundation of who we are. But here's the catch—most of us rarely step out of our comfort zones to intentionally build new relationships that could elevate our lives. Instead, we stick with the same crowd we've known for years, doing the same things we've always done. It's like staying in the same trench during a firefight; you might feel safe, but you're not advancing.

Now, there's nothing wrong with hanging out with the same crew if they're the right crew. If your circle is filled with successful, driven individuals who inspire and challenge you, chances are you'll thrive too. It's like being part of an elite unit where everyone is focused, disciplined, and pushing each other to be better. But if your friends are constantly broke, making poor financial decisions, and stuck in negative habits, what are the odds you'll break free and build wealth? It's like trying to win a firefight with a squad that's out of ammo. You're not going far.

The same goes for education and personal growth. If the people around you are unhealthy and toxic, it's unlikely you'll suddenly become successful. To level up, you've got to level up your network.

I grew up in a poor neighbourhood, and if I'd stayed in that environment, I'd probably be stuck in the same cycle of struggle. Joining the military was my ticket out in some ways. It forced me to leave behind toxic relationships and a comfort zone that was holding me back. Moving away from everything I knew was one of the hardest but most transformative decisions of my life. It gave me a new circle of people who were driven, disciplined, and focused on growth. My life has never been the same since.

Imagine two soldiers, Private Stagnant and Private Progression. Private Stagnant hangs out with a group that's always complaining, skipping PT, and blowing their paycheques on unnecessary gadgets. Private Progression, on the other hand, surrounds himself with peers who are focused on career advancement, financial stability, and personal growth. Over time, Private Progression gets promoted, saves money, and builds a solid future, while Private Stagnant stays stuck in the same cycle. Who do you want to be?

This doesn't mean abandoning your current friends entirely. Instead, push yourself outside your circle, even just a little. Attend networking events, join professional organizations, or take up a new hobby where you can meet like-minded individuals. This way, you can "average up" the five people you spend the most time with.

In the military, your squad can determine the success or failure of a mission. The same principle applies to your financial and personal growth. Surround yourself with individuals who challenge you, inspire you, and push you to reach your full potential. At the end of the day, your success is only as strong as the team you keep. The people you associate with will influence your mindset, habits, and decisions, so align yourself with those who share your drive and ambition.

This truth might hit hard for some, but it's important to remember it's okay to want more, to strive for more, and to grow beyond your current circumstances. Growth doesn't mean abandoning your friends or family; it means doing what's best for you and those closest to you. The reality is, when you're struggling or "a nobody," few people may show interest in supporting you. But when you rise and become "somebody," you'll often face criticism or envy from those who once ignored you. This is why it's crucial to build a network of like-minded individuals who genuinely want to see you succeed.

Stay focused on your mission, surround yourself with the right people, and don't let fear of judgment or change hold you back. True allies will celebrate your growth, not resent it. Your journey to success is yours alone. Choose a squad that will help you win the battle, not hold you back.

Marry For Money and Wealth

Marry for money and wealth,
and you may end up rich.

Wait! Before you start judging me, hear me out. My family didn't come from money. I'm the product of immigrant parents who arrived in Canada in the late 80s with nothing but dreams and a few suitcases. They learned the hard lessons of money through trial, error, and a lot of ramen noodles.

The financial state you're in when you pick your life partner matters a lot. If one (or both) of you is drowning in debt, student loans, credit cards, or that time you financed a jet ski, it's going to be tough to level each other up financially. Achieving financial security is a team effort. It starts with honesty, a shared vision, and a long-term perspective. If one of you is running in the wrong direction, you're both going to get lit up. Remember those wedding vows? "For richer or poorer, in sickness and in health?" Yeah, that's not just poetic, it's a financial nuclear warning label. You need to be on the same page about money.

Money discussions should be as normal as arguing over whose turn it is to take out the trash. If your partner is a drifty spender and you're a penny-pinching saver, you're going to have a bad time. Sure, opposites attract, but when it comes to money, mismatched priorities can turn your relationship into a financial dumpster fire.

When I say "marry for money," I don't mean marrying someone with a trust fund (though, hey, no judgment). I mean marrying someone who shares your mindset about money. Someone who gets that saving for retirement is just as important as that weekend getaway. Someone who understands that financial goals are a team mission, not a solo operation. Because here's the truth. If you're not aligned on money, everything you build together; your home, your dreams, your future, can vanish faster than a private's motivation after a 5 km ruck march. So, choose wisely. Marry someone who's got your back, both emotionally and financially. That way, no matter what life throws at you, you'll always have each other, and maybe even a solid retirement plan.

Time in the Market

Time in the market is your greatest ally. It's not about timing the market, but letting time work its magic.

Investing isn't about making a quick buck. There's no such thing as becoming an overnight millionaire, unless you win the lottery or marry into money (and let's be real, neither of those is a solid plan). Investing is a long, often boring process. It's slow and gradual, like waiting for your next promotion or that sweet posting to an OUTCAN. Too many people think investing is fast-paced, filled with excitement and instant rewards. But it's more like standing in line at the mess hall— you wait, you get your food, and you don't rush the cook.

The best way to beat the market? Time in the market. Like compound interest, your money grows on itself, just like a snowball rolling down hill. The longer you let it roll, the bigger it gets. And time is one of your best allies, especially if you start early.

Imagine two soldiers, Captain Early and Major Late. Captain Early starts investing $200 a month right after basic training at age twenty. Major Late, on the other hand, waits until he's forty, just a few years before retirement, to start investing the same amount. By the time they both hit sixty, Captain Early's investments have grown significantly more, thanks to those extra twenty years of compounding. Major Late? He's playing catch up, and it's not as fun as it sounds.

Investing isn't about flashy moves or trying to outsmart the market. It's about discipline, patience, and sticking to the plan, just like showing up to PT every morning, even when you'd rather sleep in. So, don't get distracted by the noise. Put your money to work, leave it alone, and let time work its magic.

And remember, the market doesn't care about your rank; it rewards consistency. So, stop waiting for the "perfect time" and start now. Your future self will thank you.

The FOMO

The distance between you and your target cannot be avoided.

Stay focused on the mission. FOMO is like that overeager recruit who rushes into a mission without a plan, pushing investors to make impulsive decisions. Chasing trendy stocks, diving into sectors they don't understand, or gambling on quick profits often leads to disaster. Take NFTs (non-fungible tokens), for example. These digital assets, representing ownership of unique items like art or virtual real estate, exploded in popularity in 2021. But let's be honest, what exactly are they? I'm still trying to figure it out myself.

Imagine paying hundreds of thousands for a virtual house in cyberspace when you could buy a real one for the same price. Sure, celebrities might be cashing in, but who's really winning here? And good luck selling that digital property later; you'll need a "real" real estate agent!

The same goes for digital art. Why spend a fortune on a virtual portrait when you could never afford a physical masterpiece by Van Gogh or Picasso? It feels like the "greater fool theory" in action. Buying something with no real value behind it and hoping to sell it to someone else at a higher price is not a smart move.

The lesson here is simple: patience and consistency win. Just like in the military, rushing into a mission without proper intel or preparation is a recipe for failure. Don't chase trends or expect overnight riches. Know what you're investing in, avoid the hype, and stick to your financial mission.

Smart decisions, not FOMO, will keep you on the path to real financial success. Stay disciplined, stay focused, and remember—the target doesn't move, so you just need to aim carefully.

Exposing the Faux Generals

Beware of self-proclaimed leaders; they'll sell you a shortcut, but leave you lost on the road.

The internet is a powerful tactical tool, but it can easily backfire if not used with caution. On one hand, it's packed with valuable information that can help you build wealth. On the other hand, it's a minefield of scams, misinformation, and shady tactics. Where you get your intel matters. Just like you wouldn't trust a random source for mission-critical information, you shouldn't trust just any website or podcast for financial advice. Reliable sources exist, but so do sketchy ones. Always cross-check your intel and never rely on a single source.

Scammers are out there, and they're using advanced tactics to exploit vulnerabilities. Think about those targeted ads that pop up after you visit a site or watch a video. They're designed to manipulate you, turning a "want" into a "need." Fraudulent influencers are no different. They build massive followings, promote overpriced products, and spread misinformation, all while pretending to be experts. Many of them are paid to push certain ideas or services, so their advice isn't always unbiased. Podcasts and online content can be informative and entertaining, but don't rely on them blindly. Popular platforms like Reddit have educated voices, but take their advice with skepticism. Verify before trusting.

Real experts like Warren Buffett or Michael Burry aren't pitching products or "secrets." They're too busy succeeding. When they share insights, it's in professional settings, not flashy ads or courses. If someone's selling the "secret" to wealth, they're likely making money off you, not their advice. Stay vigilant—gather intel from multiple sources, analyze carefully, and follow proven investors who've weathered market storms. Trust your training. Verify, analyze, and execute with precision. Real wealth comes from discipline, smart investing, and consistent effort, not quick fixes. Stay sharp, stay skeptical, and keep your financial mission on track.

Gambling: A Bet, Not a Plan

Gambling for success
is a bet, not a plan.

If you think hitting the casino will make you rich, you're playing the wrong game. Sure, going out on a Saturday night with your buddies, grabbing a few drinks, and tossing some chips on the table for fun is one thing. But when you walk into that casino, do you think you'll walk out with fast cash? That's a dangerous mindset, and believe me when I say I've been there. I used to think I had the magic formula to beat the house. Roulette? I had a "system." Slots? I was "due for a jackpot." Spoiler alert—I was wrong. Oh, so wrong. The worst part? It wasn't that I couldn't afford to lose; it was the false confidence that my steady paycheque would always bail me out. "I'll just earn it back," I told myself. Turns out, that sense of security was my downfall. I exploited it like a rookie exploiting a loophole in the regs—wrong move.

And let's not forget the emotional rollercoaster. That first jackpot? Pure adrenalin. But chasing that high? It's like trying to outrun a tornado in a golf cart; you're not winning, and it's only a matter of time before things go sideways. Gambling can mess with your mental health, strain relationships, and even lead to criminal activity. I've seen it happen. One buddy of mine got so deep into online sports betting that he started "borrowing" money from his spouse's savings to cover his losses. When the truth came out, it nearly ended his marriage and left him in a financial hole that took years to dig out of.

Gambling is not a strategy—it's a trap. These days, I stick to poker nights with friends, where the stakes are low and the laughs are high.

So, learn from this mistake. Gambling might seem like a quick fix, but it's a surefire way to blow up your finances, your mental health, and your future. Be smart, be responsible, and remember—the house always wins.

Not Saving Earlier

Regret not saving earlier?
It's the costliest mistake.

I'll admit it, I wish I'd been more mindful of my finances in my early twenties. Like many young adults, I got sidetracked, lacked financial literacy, and missed out on years of compound interest and growth. But here's the good news—it's never too late (or too early) to start saving and investing for a secure future. The key is to start early so you can harness the power of exponential growth throughout your career and beyond. Here's why starting early matters:

- **Time horizon**—the sooner you invest, the longer your money has to grow. Compound interest is like a snowball. Start early, and it'll grow exponentially over time.

- **Lower risk**—as a young CAF member, you've got time on your side. Market ups and downs won't break you because you can ride them out and invest in higher-risk, higher-reward opportunities.

- **Flexibility**—small, regular contributions add up over time, creating a financial cushion for future expenses or retirement.

- **Habits**—building good saving habits early sets you up for long-term success. Like PT, consistent effort pays off.

- **Retirement planning**—starting early means more time to accumulate wealth, making it easier to hit your retirement goals.

Small delays can have a tremendous impact on your long-term financial outcome. Don't wait! Even small steps now can lead to big wins later.

In the military, every operation teaches us something: what succeeded, what failed, and how to adapt for the next mission. Similarly, my financial missteps have been tough but valuable lessons. From overspending on unnecessary gear to neglecting savings during deployments, each misstep cost me time, money, and peace of mind. But just like in training, setbacks are opportunities to grow.

By sharing my ten biggest financial blunders, I hope to help you avoid these traps and stay on course toward your financial mission. Remember, discipline and adaptability are key. Learn from my mistakes, fortify your financial strategy, and keep advancing toward your goals.

Mission success is within reach. Act now!

AFTER ACTION REPORT

- **Overcoming personal fear is crucial when making financial decisions.** As anxiety often originates from uncertainty or past mistakes, or the lack of knowledge, it can paralyze you.

- **Emotional decision-making can derail financial progress.** Eliminating debt requires behavioural changes and strategies that reduce harmful spending and encourage healthier financial habits.

- **Hidden costs and expensive habits can consume your resources unnecessarily.** Redirect funds toward wealth building by identifying financial leaks that quietly drain your bank account. Cutting these non-essential expenses helps free up money for your financial goals.

- **Commitment to upskilling ensures long-term wealth accumulation.** Pursuing financial growth involves continuous learning, and seeking mentorship or resources enhances decision-making.

- **Avoiding common financial mistakes.** Focusing on trivial expenses that add no value distracts you from wealth-building priorities. Failing to build an effective entourage, delaying your investment journey, and gambling your money away limit growth opportunities.

People need to get financial advice. I'm not talking only about money management. You also need to have a sense of where you want to be, where you would like to live and what you would like to do once you've given up a full-time job.

DR. SHERRY COOPER
The New Retirement

CHAPTER 6

SUPPLY LINES FINITE RESOURCES

EVERY SERVICE MEMBER eventually faces their final mission order—Retirement. But unlike your typical deployment, retirement can last decades, and you're not getting orders to deploy again. The big question is—are you ready for the transition from combat boots to retirement loafers? Building wealth isn't just about saving pennies for tomorrow; it's about setting up a financial system that supports you and your family long after you've hung up your uniform and turned in your gear. A wise Sergeant and friend of mine once told me, *"Once you've turned in your beret, you're left with what you've got."* Sounds like tough love, but it's also the truth. The time to prepare is now.

Listen up! In this chapter, we're diving into the stuff you won't find in the typical field manual: Pensions, RRSPs, TFSAs, and all that financial jargon that's just as crucial to your future as any final tactical operation. We'll break down the social benefits and financial elements you'll need once you hang up the uniform and leave the frontlines. We will investigate those three facets:

1   After the Frontline: Post-Service Wealth
2   Final Line of Support: The Last Resort
3   End Mission Resources: Military Retirement Savings

What's your next line of defence? How do you prepare for the big final mission? "Retirement" doesn't just happen by accident; it requires strategy, discipline, and a bit of that military mindset. So, let's suit up, get our financial fortitude in shape, and prepare for your most rewarding mission yet—*your well-earned retirement!* Because this one's going to pay off big time.

AFTER THE FRONTLINE: POST-SERVICE WEALTH

Let's talk pension! As CAF members, you benefit from a great pension plan after you retire from your service. Immediate annuity is granted to retired military members after twenty-five years of pensionable service. That means you will receive a monthly payout for life once you've completely released from the CAF. Your annual pension benefit will be equal to about 2% per year of service to a maximum of 70% (thirty-five years of service). After twenty-five years of loyal service, you'll be able to collect a minimum of 50% of your annual income based on your best five years' average salary. Isn't it great!

CAF PAY SCALE (NON-COMMISSIONED MEMBERS)		
	SALARY	HIGHEST INCENTIVE IN THE RANK
PRIVATE	$52,044	$71,928
CORPORAL	$82,296	$88,044
MASTER-CORPORAL	$85,416	$94,092
SERGEANT	$95,508	$100,080
WARRANT OFFICER	$104,328	$107,964
MASTER WARRANT OFFICER	$116,016	$120,684
CHIEF WARRANT OFFICER	$126,744	$132,012

CAF Pay Scale as of January 1, 2026

CAF PAY SCALE (COMMISSIONED OFFICER)		
	SALARY	HIGHEST INCENTIVE IN THE RANK
CAPTAIN	$106,332	$140,544
MAJOR	$143,796	$160,220
LIEUTENANT-COLONEL	$166,644	$177,348
COLONEL	$188,208	$210,492
BRIGADIER-GENERAL	$222,780	$241,164
MAJOR-GENERAL	$255,612	$300,240
LIEUTENANT GENERAL	$328,332	$355,428

CAF Pay Scale as of January 1, 2026
All data does not include the specialist pay scale and other specific trade bonuses. For more details, see the Government of Canada website under Military Pay Scale.

Fifty percent of your best five years will ultimately become your annual income during your retirement. Now, the question is—will you be able to live on that amount only? Your cost of living may have increased or decreased depending on your situation. But realistically, the cost of living will continue to rise (just like the price of eggs that keeps hiking up), divorce could happen, kids may still live with you, and your mortgage payment may not be over yet. Will you be able to hold your desired lifestyle with half of your current income while taking care of all your expenses? If you answered "No," then you are not too far from the harsh reality for most people.

If health permits, many of you will still have a desire to travel, purchase new items, take out a loan to expand your backyard, construct a new fence or purchase a new car. Such a desire may prevent you from having sufficient savings for retirement. My top advice prior to reaching retirement is straightforward:

Save as much as you
can while you can!

Personally, I prefer to put aside between 15% and 20% of my CAF income after taxes toward my retirement fund (also invested). But if you can do more than that, do it. A big portion should go toward your retirement savings. I rarely keep more than what is required for my essentials. Most officers, after five years in the military, can easily make over six figures in annual income. And yet, after studying many people's personal finances, upper-level earners may not have as much savings as you think or may even have barely begun to own any investments that could help them supplement their pension fund. In their defence, as I mentioned earlier, they may have experienced a catastrophic event, such as divorce, or a death or health issues within their family. These can all have a direct impact on their financial situation. Those things are out of our control, but others can be attributed to what we've discussed earlier, such as a lack of financial literacy and bad habits.

You'd think it'd be easy to put away a solid chunk of your earnings when you're raking in a six-figure salary, right? Well, not exactly. The more you make, the more you tend to spend. It's like this—instead of buying just one pack of cigarettes, now you can afford two a week. Why? Purchasing power. With that nice pay raise at the start of each fiscal year, you feel like you have more room to splurge. It's easy to fall into the trap of thinking you can afford it all, but instead of socking away money and investing for the future, many people end up spending more, completely overlooking how they'll manage when it's time to retire. The focus shifts from building wealth for the long haul to enjoying the now, leaving retirement planning on the back burner.

Retirement Planning

There are a few factors that you will need to consider before your retirement to make the right decisions today. Whether you should rely on your pension alone will depend on:

1   Your retirement goals
2   The size of your pension
3   Your other sources of income

How much money you will need for your retirement will depend on your personal retirement goals. Determine early what you WANT to do or HAVE during your retirement and how much you will need to pay for it. This will help you determine how much money you will need to generate from your income sources. If your pension is the only source of income available at that time, you will have to do the math and decide on either reducing your expectations or making sure you have an additional stream of income to support your multiple projects and expected lifestyle. When you stop working, money might get tighter, so it's important to take a good look at the size of your pension and plan accordingly.

At retirement, your goals won't just depend on your pension, but also on other income sources you've built up. In addition to your CAF pension, you'll have benefits from Social Security, Old Age Security, and your own savings, investments, and RRSP. These programs will help top up your pension and provide more financial stability. But if your retirement goals are bigger than what your pension and Social Security can cover, you'll need to create extra income streams.

That's why it's a good idea to start diversifying your income years before retirement. Begin saving and investing as early as possible so that, by the time you retire, your investments are working for you. This way, you can enjoy extra income from multiple sources once you hang up the uniform. While your pension is a great safety net, relying on it alone isn't enough.

Release Section

It's a great idea to talk to an adviser about your retirement plan. The release sections are there to help guide you through the process of planning for your CAF retirement. You're in good hands with professionals who are dedicated to helping you understand your options and create a plan that works for your financial goals. I'd suggest starting your research and planning well before you start the release process. Don't wait until the final stretch of your career to gather information and plan for retirement.

It's never too early to talk to a retirement planner. Things like inflation and taxes can really affect your RRSP withdrawals and other parts of your retirement plan, so it's important to get ahead of those factors. By learning about different retirement plans, accounts, and investments now, you'll be way more prepared to make smart decisions when it's time to retire.

FINAL LINE OF SUPPORT: THE LAST RESORT

Retirement is not a right nor a guarantee. Some of us may have to continue to work longer, if not harder, to keep up with our current military lifestyle. It's not just a matter of turning sixty-five and calling it a day. For many, the rising cost of living and inflation can catch up, meaning they may need to keep working longer, or even harder, to maintain their lifestyle. It's not a surprise that some Canadians might have to work beyond sixty-five. Can you imagine—you've spent years jumping out of planes, surviving on field rations, and collecting enough broken bones (physically and emotionally) to make your body a walking VA checklist. Then, the country drops you back into "civilian life"—a world where "deployments" means online meetings, "boots on the ground" means walking through aisles of merchandise, and your new "fireteam" slash team leader is a twenty-five year-old intern who thinks that "PT" is beneath them. Starting over in this alien terrain is like being handed a map of *The Lord of the Rings*' Middle-earth and being told to navigate Afghanistan's mountainous regions blindfolded.

For CAF members, though, if you joined the Forces at twenty and retired at forty-five, you'll have a generous pension for life, which is a lot earlier than most people. But even with a pension, it's not enough to just sit back and live comfortably. You could get by, but you'd have to be incredibly frugal, especially as the cost of living keeps going up. If your pension becomes your only source of income, things could get tight. You've survived sandstorms, overnight guard duty, and living on rations for three months, but are you built for this sort of chaos?

The CAF Pension is Not Guaranteed

Not everyone will qualify for this pension, and yes, you heard that right. If you joined late, keep in mind: to unlock the immediate annuity and receive a lifetime pension, you must complete twenty-five years of continuous service.

If you leave before meeting this requirement, or if you joined after age thirty-six, you likely won't be eligible for the lifetime pension. Instead, you may receive a lump sum, which is typically far less than what you'd get through lifetime payments, especially if you live long enough. It's something to consider and plan for carefully. The worst-case scenario is outliving the lump sum (most likely) you receive and not having enough to sustain yourself in old age. Unless you are released for medical reasons, but that's another topic altogether.

Canadian Social Benefits

For most Canadians, the Old Age Security (OAS) pension is the main income once they retire. As of January to March 2025, if you're between sixty-five and seventy-four, the maximum you can get is $727.67 a month, which adds up to about $8,732 a year. If you're seventy-five or older, you'll get a little over $800.44 per month, or $9,605 per year. But here's the catch—the OAS is income-tested. If your annual net world income is above a certain amount, you might have to pay some of it back. If you made over $148,451 in 2024 (for those aged 65—74) or $154,196 (for those 75+), you could face a clawback.

No, for real! Living on that amount is tough! When you're looking at $8,732 to $9,605 a year, especially after living with the lifestyle the military provides, it's not exactly going to turn your retirement into a dream vacation. And if your spouse isn't working, you're basically cutting that amount in half. You can't depend on your government pension to fund your golden years. That's why I can't stress enough how important it is to start planning. Build up your investments and create other income streams now. Whether it's building a dividend portfolio or getting into real estate, start securing your future before you retire from the Forces. You've trained for your mission, now it's time to train for your retirement!

MAXIMUM PAYMENTS AND INCOME THRESHOLDS		
AGE	MAXIMUM MONTHLY PAYMENT AMOUNT	TO RECEIVE THE OAS, YOUR ANNUAL NET WORLD INCOME IN 2024
65 to 74	$727.67	Less than $148,196
75 and over	$800.44	Less than $154,196

OAS Pension Amount, January to March 2025

Rise in Cost and Reality Check

The cost of living is climbing faster than a Sergeant Major's blood pressure when you forget to shine your boots. In 2022, the consumer price index (CPI), which tracks how much things are costing, hit 8.1%, and inflation has been on the rise ever since. Prices are soaring, and it feels like we're still reeling from the 2008 housing crash. From skyrocketing grocery bills to painful excursions to the gas station, it's hard to keep up. Supply chain disruptions, labour shortages, and a housing market that's out of control are making it worse. Then, throw in the chaos of the COVID-19 pandemic and current global political tensions, and it's clear things aren't slowing down anytime soon. It's like being on a mission where every step forward is met with a new obstacle, making it tough to stay on course.

Now, here's the reality check! Once you retire, your pay is going to get cut in half. That generous pension you're counting on is based on an average of your top five years of salary, and it's not going to keep you living the high life. If you want to keep living comfortably, like you did in your thirties and forties (without scrambling for loose change), you need assets to back you up. You've got to build something beyond your paycheque now, whether it's through investments, real estate, or a solid dividend portfolio. Don't wait until the last minute to figure this out. Set yourself up now so when it's time to retire, you're not running on fumes. Keep your future mission in mind. You've got this!

About to Retire?

Alright, so you're looking down the barrel of retirement, whether you're just about to hang up the uniform or you've recently done it. First off, congrats! You've earned it. No more Personal Annual Report (PAR) to conduct, no more Annual Fitness Test to pass, and no more annual mandatory online courses to complete. But now, the big question— what's next?

Is your pension going to cover your lifestyle, or are you going to be digging through your old kit bag for spare change? Here's the thing—it's not too late to improve your financial situation, but you're not going to suddenly strike it rich by next Tuesday, either. If you're a few years out from retirement, now's the time to get serious about boosting your income streams. I get it, after decades of service, the last thing you want to do is work harder. But hear me out— building wealth now, even at the tail end of your career, is better than doing nothing and hoping everything magically works out.

Let's say you've already started putting some money aside; good start, but it's time to step up your game. If you haven't yet, perhaps investigate dividend-paying stocks. The beauty of these is that they pay you back regularly, like a solid paycheque, just without the drill Sergeant yelling at you to wake up at 0500. I'm personally invested in a solid dividend portfolio that regularly gives me passive income. This means while I'm sitting back enjoying some downtime, the money is still working for me. Real estate's another good option. If you can manage a rental property or two, those monthly rent payments can help top up your income and keep you comfortable without breaking a sweat.

Now, don't expect to roll in cash overnight. You're not going to make up for decades of missed opportunity in one or two years. But if you start now, you can still make strides. Look! A little effort now can go a long way in securing a decent retirement. You won't be living like you're back in your twenties, but you won't be scraping by either. Whether it's finding a side hustle, building up a real estate portfolio, or jumping into dividend investing, just do something. Even a small shift can make a massive difference down the road.

Here's another idea—if you can't lower your expenses, consider relocating somewhere where your money stretches further. There are places with much lower costs of living that could really make your pension go a long way. I know people who've retired abroad and are loving life. Take my buddy Sgt Travelalot, for example. He's doing great with his pension.

He saved up, sold his house, and cashed in on some liquidity. It's not for everyone, though. Not everyone wants to pick up and start fresh in a new country. But for those who are open to it, it can be a solid option.

Of course, it depends on your situation. Personally, moving to somewhere like Thailand doesn't appeal to me. The heat would be unbearable, and I love my four seasons! Plus, I can't imagine asking my parents to travel all that way just for me. It's all about what works best for you.

Personally, I think Ontario would be the prime choice. The reason has to do with tax implications and proximity. The income taxes are lower than in other provinces, and it's closer to my family as well. It would make sense that you use your last posting relocation benefit (yes, CAF members get that one last relocation benefit) to move you free of charge to your retirement location. So, picking a province with a lower tax income bracket for your main residence makes absolute sense (don't forget that your pension is still taxable income). Because if you are like me, you'd probably be travelling half of the year at retirement anyway. Therefore, a cabin on a lake will suffice.

The bottom line? It's never too late to take control of your financial future. Put in the work now, and when retirement rolls around, you'll be able to relax and enjoy it without stressing about what comes next.

END MISSION RESOURCES:
MILITARY RETIREMENT SAVINGS

Alright, we've talked about this before, but let's target the RRSP again. I know "retirement" might feel like it's lightyears away, especially when you're still up at 0500 answering to the command (and let's face it, probably still half asleep). But trust me, the sooner you start saving, the easier your transition to post-service life will be, and you won't have to worry about your bank account while you're enjoying your well-deserved retirement.

Think of an RRSP as your financial grenade. You pull the pin now, and it grows on its own until you need it. Here's the truth—the government gives you a little reward when you contribute. You throw in $5,000? Boom, your taxable income just dropped by $5,000. How's that for a win? And then there's the magic of compound interest. Your money is making more money while you're busy with other stuff. It won't happen overnight, but over time, it adds up like deployment pay. The longer you let it grow, the better off you'll be when it's time to kick back and relax in retirement, without needing to live off your old boots (figuratively, of course).

Now, we don't get employer contributions like some civilians might, and the Department of National Defence isn't matching our RRSP contributions, but it's still a solid move for your future. Plus, once it's in there, you can't touch it until retirement, which means no impulse buys when you're eyeing that new gadget for your man cave (or lady lair).

The best part? You have a ton of options on where to invest your RRSP money. This includes stocks, bonds, mutual funds, and more. Just make sure you chat with a financial adviser to figure out what works best for you. You're in charge of your future, so start saving and investing now and make sure you're ready when that final posting comes.

The End Game

Retirement isn't just about surviving when you hang up your uniform. It's about thriving. While you're in the service, that steady paycheque helps cover expenses and lets you enjoy life. But when that paycheque stops, it's essential that your finances don't hit a dead end. That's why planning and saving for retirement is critical. If you rely only on your CAF pension, you might not be able to maintain the lifestyle you had while serving. Want to travel, enjoy fine dining, or splurge on something special? You'll need more than just your pension to make that happen. Personally, I see my retirement as an opportunity to travel the world with my spouse, dine at world-class restaurants, and live without financial worries. When you're in places like Paris, the last thing you want is to wonder if you can afford your next meal.

But everyone's retirement looks different. Some might want a quiet life by the lake or more time with family, and that's perfectly fine too. Regardless of your vision, planning early gives you more options down the line. The sooner you start investing, the more you can build wealth, which is the key to financial freedom in retirement. Saving for retirement can offer several benefits.

- **Alpha**: it ensures you have enough funds to cover your living expenses once you're no longer receiving a paycheque.

- **Bravo**: it helps you maintain or upgrade your lifestyle. Without enough savings, your options are limited.

Additionally, building your retirement savings early provides security and flexibility. A well-established nest egg acts as a financial cushion for the unforeseen and gives you more control over decisions like travelling or working a bit longer if needed. The goal is to reduce your reliance on the CAF pension and other social benefits, which may not be enough to fully support your needs. By building multiple income streams now, whether through dividends, real estate, or other types of investment, you'll set yourself up for a worry-free retirement.

In my experience, creating a dividend portfolio has been a game-changer. I receive quarterly payments, and I don't have to work for them. They just parachute into my bank account. I've also previously invested in rental properties, which generate steady income each month. These investments allow you to enjoy retirement without constantly watching your bank account. The key is to diversify your income sources now so you can fully enjoy your retirement later.

AFTER ACTION REPORT

- **Financial stability post-service starts with clear retirement planning.** Identify your personal goals, align them with your pension and other sources of income, and apply proactive wealth management practices to ensure long-term financial security.

- **Understand available resources at retirement to counter unforeseen challenges.** Prepare for life's uncertainties with backup options, like your pension fund, RRSP, investments and social security benefits to create a reliable buffer for navigating money crises effectively.

- **Ensure CAF retirement safety with preparedness.** Assess your retirement savings, including CAF pensions and RRSP contributions, to confirm preparedness. Regular contributions during service, combined with leveraging tax benefits, will help grow your retirement fund, securing financial stability for life after service.

*Surround yourself with those
who challenge, inspire, and
complement your strengths. With the
right people, success is inevitable.*

CHAPTER 7

COMMAND
AND ALLIANCE
MONEY PARTNERS

IN THE MILITARY, every mission requires a solid plan, a reliable team, and good intel. Managing your finances is no different. You wouldn't go into a mission without the right squad or strategy, so why approach your financial future without the right people and tools? Take a financial adviser as your mission planner. They provide expertise and strategy to help you achieve your goals. But building a strong financial team goes beyond finding the right adviser. It's about trust, communication, and aligning with those who share your financial vision. Let's break down three key components to help you lead your financial mission with confidence:

1 Leading Your Team: How to Work with Your Adviser
2 Assembling Your Team: Picking the Right Squad
3 Clear Comms: Open Lines of Communication

At the end of this chapter, you'll have everything you need to assemble a strong financial team, communicate clearly, and execute your plan. Just like teamwork is crucial on the field, it's equally important when it comes to managing your finances.

LEADING YOUR TEAM:
HOW TO WORK WITH YOUR ADVISER

Identify and collaborate with financial advisers who align with your mission, just as you'd select the right team for a critical operation.

When I first joined the military, I was assigned to a section led by Sergeant Dowitright, a seasoned leader who had seen it all. At the time, I was green, unsure of myself, and still figuring out what it meant to lead. Sergeant Dowitright didn't just bark orders—he led by example. He was the first one on the field and the last one to leave. He took the time to teach not just the "how" but the "why" behind every decision. His calmness under pressure, his ability to adapt, and his remarkable commitment to his team left a lasting impression on me.

One moment stands out—during a high-stakes training exercise, our team was falling apart under pressure. Instead of yelling, Sergeant Dowitright pulled us aside and said, "Leadership isn't about being in charge, it's about taking care of those in your charge." That enlightening phrase shifted my entire perspective. I began to emulate his approach, putting my team first, staying calm in chaos, and always striving to lead with integrity.

Now, Sergeant Dowitright was the kind of leader who rarely raised his voice. In fact, he was so calm most of the time that when he did raise his voice, you knew you'd messed up big time. It was like hearing a librarian suddenly yell—it was so rare that it hit you like the sound of an F-18 passing by way too low. I remember one time when a teammate forgot to secure a piece of equipment, and Sergeant Dowitright let out this deep, booming "What were you thinking?!" that could've woken up the entire base. We all froze, and I swear even the birds stopped chirping. But even in those moments, there was a lesson: accountability matters, and mistakes have consequences.

That foundation he helped me build is the core of who I am as a leader today. And the same principle applies to leading a financial team—you don't follow someone who hasn't walked the path. Just as I looked to Sergeant Dowitright for guidance, I now seek out mentors who've achieved the financial success I aspire to. It's about learning from those who've already blazed the trail, whether on the battlefield or in the world of finance.

To Lead, You Must Follow First

Too many people seek advice from folks offering opinions rather than real, battle-tested insights. My advice? Find people who've been through the tough stuff and come out the other side successful. Don't be afraid to reach out and take the shot! A lot of people miss opportunities simply because they don't ask the right questions or seek the right people. One call, one conversation with the right person could unlock opportunities worth thousands, maybe even millions.

Success leaves a trail, just like boot marks on the ground. Look for the ones who've already been where you want to go and surround yourself with them. It's true what they say: "Your network is your net worth," or "You are the sum of the five people you spend the most time with." These aren't just catchy phrases—they're keys to success. Ask yourself— who can you connect with who's already winning in the area you're focusing on? Seek out those who've done it and learn from their experience. Success doesn't come from luck— it's about consistent progress and smart action. There's no shortage of books on financial success, but the one thing all successful people share is that they show up and put in the work every single day, no matter the circumstances.

ASSEMBLING YOUR TEAM:
PICKING THE RIGHT SQUAD

Discover how to surround yourself with the right people, whether it's advisers, family, or mentors, who can support your financial goals.

Just as you'd consult a weather forecaster before a mission or a medic when you're injured, getting your finances in order requires the expertise of a financial specialist. You wouldn't trust just anyone with your gear or mission planning, so why would you trust just anyone with your money? A skilled financial adviser is like a battle-tested SME—they know the terrain, have the intel, and possess the tools to help you succeed.

Think of working with a financial adviser as leading a squad. Each member has a role. Yours? It's to focus on your mission (your career and personal goals), while they handle the financial logistics. But just like any operation, you need to understand the plan and the costs up front. If your adviser isn't transparent about fees, it's like heading into an LZ without an extraction plan. Risky and potentially disastrous. Here's what to watch for when it comes to fees, because every mission has its costs:

- **Hourly rates**—like your time in the field, your adviser's time is valuable. Know their hourly rate if they charge this way.

- **Commissions**—this is the "commissioned officer" of fees. Understand if they earn based on trades and ensure they're not pushing unnecessary ones.

- **Trading fees**—these are like the cost of ammo. Every trade has a price. Know what you're paying per transaction.

- **Flat upfront fee**—some advisers charge a lump sum, like prepping for a long deployment. Confirm what's included and if there are hidden costs.

- **Annual retainer fees**—think of this as a maintenance fee for keeping your financial plan operational. Be clear on recurring costs.

- **Hidden fees**—these are like running out of rations mid-mission. Unexpected and frustrating. Scrutinize the fine print to avoid surprises.

Just as you'd never launch an operation without full intel, don't commit to a financial strategy without understanding the costs. Review your adviser's fee structure thoroughly, and don't just skim it like a quick reconnaissance. Ask questions, demand clarity, and ensure you're making an informed decision.

In short, your financial future is too important to leave to chance. Choose the right adviser, understand their fees, keep your finances as sharp as your kit, and always trust your instincts. If something feels off, it probably is. No one knows your mission better than you.

What To Seek in Your Partnership

Before a financial planner can craft a solid strategy, they need to understand your mission. What are you trying to achieve with your money? A top-tier adviser will take the time to learn about your priorities, risk tolerance, and long-term goals. Are you aiming for stability, growth, or high-risk, high-reward opportunities? Your adviser should align their strategy with your unique situation, helping you to not only meet, but also exceed your financial targets. You wouldn't go in without a clear objective, and neither should your adviser.

Financial Status Evaluation

Once your adviser understands your goals, they'll conduct a thorough assessment of your current financial position. Here's what they'll need to know:

- **Assets and liabilities**—what's in your kit? This includes your savings, investments, property, and debts. Knowing both sides of the equation is critical for building a solid plan.

- **Sources of income**—where's the cash coming from? Whether it's military pay, secondary jobs, or investments, understanding your income streams helps determine how much you can allocate toward your goals.

- **Spending vs. saving**—are you living lean or indulging in extras? Your adviser will analyze your spending habits to identify areas for improvement, like cutting unnecessary expenses and boosting savings.

- **Special circumstances**—every mission has unique challenges. Do you have dependents, health needs, or other financial considerations? Your adviser needs this intel to tailor a plan that fits your life.

By gathering this information, your adviser can create a clear picture of your financial landscape and design a strategy to bridge the gap between where you are and where you want to go.

Crafting a Customized Plan

A solid financial plan is like a mission blueprint; it outlines the steps needed to achieve your objectives. Your adviser will address critical questions, such as:

- **How much should I save while working?** This is your "supply drop" for the future.

- **What type of investment accounts should I use?** From TFSA, RRSP and others. Your adviser shall recommend the best options based on tax implications and growth potential.

- **How should I invest my money?** This is your "battle strategy." Should you focus on stocks, bonds, or a balanced mix? Your adviser shall tailor an investment approach to your risk tolerance and goals.

- **What insurance do I need?** Just like you wouldn't go into combat without the right gear, your adviser shall help you determine which insurance policies are essential.

- **When can I retire?** This is your "end game." Your adviser should be able to map out an estimated timeline to financial freedom.

- **How much can I spend in retirement?** Knowing your operational range ensures you don't run out of resources.

- **When should I claim Social Security?** Timing is critical. Your adviser shall help you maximize your benefits.

Portfolio Design

Your investment portfolio is your tactical gear. It needs to be well-rounded and diversified. Your adviser should help you build a mix of assets (stocks, bonds, real estate, etc.) that minimizes risk and maximizes returns. They'll also guide you on the best accounts to use, ensuring tax efficiency and avoiding unnecessary fees. This is like choosing the right base for your operations: secure, efficient, and mission ready.

Strategic Withdrawal

Just as every mission requires a careful extraction plan, your investment withdrawals need a tactical approach. Your adviser should help you determine how much you can safely withdraw each year without depleting your resources. They'll also map out the best order to pull from your accounts, minimizing taxes and penalties. It's all about maintaining a position of strength without surprises—just smooth operations.

Continuous Engagement

A great financial adviser isn't just a one-time strategist—they're your ongoing mission commander. They should regularly rebalance your portfolio, ensuring it stays aligned with your goals. This process is like adjusting your strategy based on real-time intel by optimizing gains and minimizing costs. With continuous management, you can focus on your military career and personal life, knowing your financial future is in capable hands. Who knows, they might even become your best friend! No soldier wins a war alone. Stack your roster with pros. SISIP's your lifeline, and banks are your flank cover, so use them. Financial readiness can also be a team sport.

Just as a well-executed mission leaves nothing to chance, a solid financial plan ensures your future is secure. With the right adviser, clear goals, and a disciplined strategy, you can achieve the retirement lifestyle you've worked so hard for. Trust your team, stay focused, and execute your financial mission with confidence.

Do You Need an Expert?

Should you hire a financial adviser? Well, that depends on your goals and comfort level with the fees. If you're short on time but have the budget for it, an adviser could be a good option. They'll guide you through the market's ups and downs, much like a battle buddy has your back in the field. But just like we don't follow orders blindly, don't hire an adviser without doing your homework.

One thing to keep in mind—the cost. Over time, adviser fees can really add up. For instance, if you're paying 1% annually on a $500,000 portfolio, that's $5,000 a year. If your portfolio grows at 7%, you could pay tens of thousands in fees. It's like hiring a personal trainer—you get help, but they take a piece of the gains. Make sure you're okay with that price before moving forward.

Don't rush into it just because someone looks the part. You wouldn't jump into a mission without the intel, right? Shop around, meet a few advisers, and find one whose approach fits your needs. Your financial future is too important to trust someone without asking the right questions.

Also, keep an eye out for conflicts of interest. Advisers are supposed to be objective, but some may have financial incentives that influence their recommendations. Think of it like a supply Sergeant who always pushes the same gear—it may be good, but it might not be the best for your mission. If something feels off, ask for clarification. It's your money, and you deserve to know where it's going and why.

Lastly, don't rely on just one source. You wouldn't go into battle with only one piece of intel, right? If your adviser's advice doesn't sit well with you, or if they're hard to reach, that's a red flag. You need someone invested in your long-term goals, not just collecting fees.

At the end of the day, working with a financial adviser can be a solid move, especially if you're new to investing. But always remember it's your money. Take control, educate yourself, and make sure the advice you get aligns with your best interests. Just like you wouldn't go into battle blind, don't go into investing without the knowledge to back up your decisions.

My Personal Take on Advisers

Personally, I'm not a fan of hefty annual fees, especially when they're not tied to advisers' performance. You see, no matter if your portfolio is gaining or losing over time, regardless of the performance of your unrealized capital gains, the broker or adviser will still charge you money for management fees. It feels like paying for ammo I might never use, just sitting there collecting dust. I'd rather invest that cash myself! Plus, I enjoy being hands-on, researching sectors, picking investments, and actively managing my portfolio. But that's just my style.

Now, I'm not saying you should skip expert advice, but I want to encourage you to take control of your financial future. The more you understand about investing, the better equipped you'll be to make decisions that align with your goals. If you enjoy getting into the numbers, you can absolutely steer your financial journey yourself.

Financial advisers and institutions usually cater to a broad range of clients, so their advice may not always be tailored to your unique situation. What works for one person might not work for you. That's why it's so important to really understand the advice you're given. If anything feels off, don't hesitate to ask for clarification.

Before consulting with an adviser, spend some time learning the basics of finance. The more informed you are, the more confident you'll be when making decisions. Knowledge is power, and it's one of the best investments you can make. So, always do your research, question assumptions, and make sure you're comfortable with the strategy before handing over your hard-earned money.

CLEAR COMMS: OPEN LINES OF COMMUNICATION

In the battlefield of life, the more
you communicate, the fewer surprises
you'll face in the financial warzone.

Clear communication is key, whether you're heading into a mission or tackling family finances. In the military, you wouldn't go into an operation without briefing your team, and the same applies to your financial life.

Whether it's on the field or at home, communication is important. Yet, when it comes to discussing finances with family and dependents, this often becomes a challenge. Many Canadians, especially in military families, shy away from these conversations, leaving financial matters to be handled in isolation or behind closed doors. The truth? If you don't communicate openly with your loved ones about finances, you risk the future stability of your family.

For many people, especially in cultures with deeply ingrained taboos, talking about finances is about as comfortable as sharing a trench with your enemy. I know this firsthand. Growing up in an Asian family, there were three things that were off-limits at the dinner table: sex, health, and finances. You didn't ask about money, you didn't discuss health issues, and sex, well, that wasn't even acknowledged until you were well into adulthood, if at all. Everything was hidden beneath a thick haze of silence, and the mere suggestion of discussing money was met with looks of shame or irritation. It's not that my family didn't care; it's just that it was culturally ingrained to keep such matters private, often because financial discussions were seen as a sign of weakness or failure.

However, as I grew older and started navigating the world on my own, I quickly realized that keeping quiet about money was a dangerous game. In the military, we understand that clear communication can mean the difference between life and death. The same applies to family finances. When you fail to communicate, you risk leaving your loved ones unprepared for financial emergencies, or worse, a future without a solid financial plan.

In military terms, failing to communicate your financial position to your dependents is like entering a combat zone without a map or a plan. You wouldn't do that on a mission, so why do it in life? The risks are just as real: debt, financial instability, and missed opportunities.

Of course, approaching the subject of money can be awkward at first. Just like that first time you were in a briefing room with your CO, feeling out of your element, talking about finances with family may feel uncomfortable. But the more you do it, the easier it gets. Start small. Share your goals, your financial priorities, and the realities you're facing. It's not about perfection; it's about preparing your loved ones for the future. Just as you would prepare your team for a mission. I know it may not be easy, especially if you're coming from a background where finances were shrouded in secrecy, but remember, financial transparency in the family isn't a weakness, it's a strength. And sometimes, just like in the military, the toughest conversations are the ones that end up saving the most lives.

We live by the creed of leaving no one behind. The same principle applies to your family and your financial legacy. Building wealth isn't just about securing your own future. It's about creating opportunities for the next generation too. Whether it's funding your children's education, leaving a legacy for your spouse, or ensuring your family's financial security, your actions today will echo for years to come.

Early on, I focused only on my financial goals, but when I heard a fellow officer talk about setting up an education fund for his kids I realized I needed to broaden my scope. Although I don't have children yet, this insight has made me rethink my approach. I'm now actively preparing for my future family, setting up the foundations that will ensure I can provide a solid financial start for our future kids.

Remember, wealth building is a team effort. Your family is your support system, and involving them in your financial plans ensures that you're not only building wealth but also a legacy of financial resilience and security. Just like in the field, you'll get much farther with your team by your side.

AFTER ACTION REPORT

- **Choose the right financial team for success.** Pick advisers whose values and goals align with yours. Choose those who genuinely care about your future and have the expertise to guide you toward your financial objectives.

- **Build your financial entourage and optimize your support.** Seek out experienced individuals who have been where you want to go. Successful people leave a trail. Connect with them and learn from their journey.

- **Keep your comms clear at home for less vulnerability.** Financial silence within a family leads to confusion and leaves everyone exposed. Open conversations about money, goals, and planning turn your household into a mission-ready unit. The more your loved ones know, the better prepared they'll be for life's battle.

- **Share what you've learned to help others grow.** Teaching your family and peers about financial discipline is a legacy move. Share what you've learned, lead by example, and help others rise. That's how real leaders build strong communities, both in uniform and beyond.

- **Your money, your mission, your move.** Whether you use an adviser or go solo, take ownership. Keep learning, ask questions, and stay engaged. You're in command, making your financial choices with intention and confidence.

CHAPTER 8

MISSION ACCOMPLISHED
WEALTH-BUILDING TO
FINANCIAL SUCCESS

FINANCIAL INDEPENDENCE BEGINS with education, disciplined savings, and smart investments. It's about building wealth beyond a pension, with long-term strategies like real estate, stocks, and bonds. Patience and consistency are essential to win the financial war.

In combat, we all know the drill—no battle plan survives first contact with the enemy. Similarly, even the best investment strategy needs constant evaluation and adjustments based on real-world performance. So, just like after a mission, you must assess and adjust your financial strategies regularly. Adapting your portfolio for growth is where the magic happens and financial freedom is born.

Financial freedom hands you the reins to pick your next mission without money stress. Whether it's securing your family's future, pursuing a dream, or launching a new venture, it's your call. Mission accomplished is when you carve out your own version of financial independence, blaze your trail to victory, and set the stage to give back while paving the road for the next generation.

Success is part of the mission. The real deal is turning around to lift others. It's also about mentoring, opening doors, creating opportunities, and sharing your experiences. Financial success is bigger than you, than a bank account— it's about leaving a legacy of solid ground for future warriors.

In this chapter, we'll focus on the following:

1 After Action Report: Financial Review
2 Path to Victory: Defining Financial Independence
3 Philanthropic Operations: Giving Back
4 Enduring Mission: Custodians of Financial Prosperity

Shall we start lighting the way?

AFTER ACTION REPORT: FINANCIAL REVIEW

Assess, adapt, and move forward. Your investment portfolio is your tactical operation. Each asset is like a soldier with a specific role to play. Your strategy is your battle plan. Take the example of a service member I know. He invested heavily in one stock, treating it like a high-risk, high-reward recon mission. It looked promising at first, but the lack of diversification left him exposed when the market shifted— like being ambushed with no backup. It's a lesson learned the hard way.

To conduct your After Action Report (AAR), start by reviewing your objectives. Did your investments hit their targets? Identify your wins—like an ETF that performed steady over time—and your losses—like impulsive trades that pulverized your resources. Think about the intelligence behind your decisions. Were they based on solid research? Or did you take a gamble? Adjust your strategy as needed, just like you'd tweak your tactics after a training exercise.

Rebalance your portfolio, cut underperforming assets, and reinforce positions that show promise.

Tactical Evaluation

To really understand where you stand, assess your current financial health. Here's what to review:

- **Latest income**—how much cash is coming in right now, from your pay and any incentives?

- **Investment allocation**—where's your money going? Are you diversifying?

- **Cash flow and returns**—how's your portfolio performing? Are you seeing solid returns or feeling stuck in the mud?

This data will give you a clear picture of what's working and where you need to improve.

Pivoting When Terrain Shifts

Once you've assessed your performance, it's time to adapt. Flexibility in the military is key to overcoming the unexpected, and the same goes for your financial strategy. If one investment underperforms, don't panic. Instead, ask yourself if it's a temporary setback or a deeper issue. For example, a veteran I know invested in real estate. When the market slowed, he shifted gears—just like switching from an offensive to a defensive position—by moving into dividend-paying stocks for stable cash flow. Diversification is your force multiplier. You wouldn't go into combat relying on one tactic, so don't put all your money into one investment. Spread your assets across stocks, bonds, real estate, and other vehicles to minimize risk. Regularly review your portfolio to ensure it's in line with your goals and risk tolerance. If things aren't working, adjust.

The goal is to boost profitability and growth while minimizing financial risks. Assess what's not working, and pivot to a course of action that improves your financial situation.

Planning for Future Operations

Once you've adapted your strategy, set your sights on the next mission. Every successful mission starts with a clear objective. Define your short-term, mid-term, and long-term goals like preparing for a new deployment. A short-term goal might be building your emergency fund (think of it as your financial rucksack), while a long-term goal could be retiring comfortably (your "end of mission"). Break down these goals into actionable steps. If saving for a house is your next mission, calculate how much to set aside each month and identify investments that'll get you there. Use budgeting tools or consult with a financial adviser to stay on track. Anticipate obstacles, just as you would plan for contingencies in the field. Market downturns or unexpected expenses could be waiting for you, so build a buffer into your plan. By regularly reviewing your financial operations, you'll stay mission ready and lower your risk of financial exposure disaster. The goal isn't perfection, but progress.

Maintain a Healthy Financial Board

I've worked with CAF members who've been in the line of duty for twenty to twenty-five years yet still struggle financially. Even after decades of service, some can barely cover their basic needs, let alone build wealth. Their debts exceed their income, and they've accumulated stuff, furniture, electronics, and even storage units, which are draining their resources. In some cases, life events like a nasty divorce have thrown everything off track. Many of you may know someone whose finances crumbled after a major life change.

That's why you must stay on top of your finances, just like you do with your gear. You never know what life will throw your way. Make sure to set aside a portion of your income for emergencies and long-term goals. If financial struggles do arise, that emergency fund will be a lifeline to cover bills, pay for essentials, or deal with unexpected costs. If managing your money feels overwhelming, don't hesitate to get help. Seek guidance from a financial planner or accountant who can assist you in organizing your finances.

PATH TO VICTORY: DEFINING FINANCIAL INDEPENDENCE

We live by a code—Mission first, people always. But once the mission is complete, the target shifts. For many of us in uniform, that end goal is not just financial stability, but financial freedom. This is the state where money no longer dictates your choices. It's the place where your wealth is built, protected, and working for you, allowing you to live life on your own terms. But how does that look once you've achieved it? What does financial freedom mean after twenty-five years of service, dedication, and sacrifice?

Financial freedom is built on education and wealth accumulation through sharp investments. Those steady, disciplined moves that spark income streams beyond your salary or pension. In the military, you're trained to make strategic decisions, whether it's in combat or planning logistics, you name it. That same strategic mindset applies to wealth building. The key is long-term, consistent investments that appreciate and compound. Achieving financial freedom is like executing a successful military operation; it requires careful planning, discipline, and time. Victory is not instant, but with consistent effort and the right tactics, you can secure your financial future. You just need to map out your goals, execute your plan, and consistently adapt to challenges along the way.

So, you've put in the years, saved wisely, invested in stocks, bonds, real estate, or other income-generating assets. You've remained steady to your mission, reinvesting your gains, juggling deployments, and holding down your responsibilities at home. After retiring from active service, you have the financial cushion to call your next shots. Perhaps you've built up a rental property portfolio, generating passive income each month, allowing you to live without leaning on your pension alone. Maybe you've established an investment portfolio that continues to grow, providing you with capital to start a new business or travel the world without financial worries.

For military families, financial freedom means not just securing your own future but also empowering your children to thrive and live their best lives without the constant burden of debt or financial instability. It's about ensuring that they have the resources to pursue their dreams, whether it's higher education, starting a business, or buying their first home.

Financial freedom after service means living beyond your pension. It's waking up each day knowing that your money is working for you, not the other way around. It's the confidence to make choices that align with your values, whether that's spending time with family, investing in a new venture, or simply enjoying the fruits of your labour.

Like any successful military operation, financial freedom is the result of careful planning and execution, and consistent effort. You've done your duty. Now's the time for your money to serve you. After years of hard work, discipline, and strategic planning, you've earned the right to enjoy the fruits of your labour. The choice is yours! Travel the world, indulge in unforgettable dining experiences, and do all the things you've dreamed of without the weight of financial stress holding you back. Why? Because you levelled up. You planned. You invested wisely.

After a successful mission, you take time to regroup, reflect, and celebrate the wins. This is your moment to do the same. You've built a solid financial foundation, and now it's time to live life on your terms. Whether it's exploring new destinations, treating yourself to luxury, or simply enjoying peace of mind, you've earned it.

So, what's your next mission? Whatever it is, you're ready because you've prepared, you've executed, and now you're reaping the rewards. *Go out there and make it count!*

PHILANTHROPIC OPERATIONS: GIVING BACK

Once you've achieved financial success, it's time to widen the scope. Military service has always been about something bigger than just us, and financial success is your launchpad to pay it forward. As CAF leaders, you have a responsibility and a duty to share the knowledge you've picked up throughout your career. Helping others climb to their own financial high ground doesn't just lift them, it makes our whole community tougher. Lead by example, from the front, teach younger soldiers about financial discipline, strategic planning, and building wealth while serving.

Philanthropy isn't just about writing checks. It's about allocating your time, resources, and knowledge to make an impact and spark real change. Whether mentoring, creating opportunities, or supporting causes that align with your values, your actions can create ripples that last. It's a cycle of empowerment that keeps on going way past your watch.

For me, giving back means sharing the lessons I've learned. Writing this book is my shot at handing you the playbook. These are the strategies and insights you can run with. In the CAF, we're all about preparing the next wave of leaders. Financial empowerment fuels the same idea. By educating those coming up the ranks, we're not just building a future of service, we're locking in financial security and prosperity for the long fight. So, keep the momentum going.

In the military, we never leave a comrade behind. The same applies to your family. Building wealth isn't just about your future; it's about creating opportunities for the next generation coming behind us. Whether funding education, leaving a legacy, or ensuring financial security, your actions today will have a lasting impact. *Ready to pass on the torch?*

Great leaders aren't the ones with the most followers—they're the ones who create the most leaders.

PATRICK BET-DAVID
Valuetainment

ENDURING MISSION: CUSTODIANS OF FINANCIAL PROSPERITY

For most of us, it's never been about the fame; it's always been about the mission. And that mission? It never stops. You wrap up one operation, and you're already gearing up for the next. The same goes for your finances. Achieving financial success is just the beginning. The real fight is the next phase, preserving that success, expanding it, defending it, and ensuring that the generations after you can build on the foundation you've laid.

Generational wealth isn't just about passing down money— it's about passing on the wisdom, the discipline, the know-how to protect it and grow it. It's making sure that your children know how to use the resources you've left them, whether through investments, education, or business. This is the true meaning of legacy. Something that will carry them forward far beyond what you could ever imagine.

Most of us in the CAF won't have statues erected in our honour. We won't see our names etched in history. But we have something far more powerful to leave behind. Something that speaks louder than any medal or accolade: a legacy. A legacy that gives our children opportunities we never had, whether that's the best education, the means to start their own business, or the freedom to live without financial stress.

Building generational wealth means giving your family the chance to thrive without fear. The mission doesn't end when you retire. It's not over until the future you've secured for them stands strong. That's your real legacy. Arming your loved ones to win their own battles.

True financial success isn't
just about what we've built;
it's about what we leave behind.

AFTER ACTION REPORT

- **Financial independence is the freedom to choose how you live and control your time.** It's built through education, disciplined saving, and smart, consistent investments. With a solid plan, you gain the freedom to choose your next mission on your own terms.

- **Mission review is critical to progress.** Assess your income, investments, and returns. What worked, what didn't, and why. If something underperformed, pivot and adapt. Rebalance your portfolio, diversify, and make sure your strategy still aligns with your goals.

- **True wealth carries responsibility.** Share your knowledge, mentor others, and lead by example. True leadership creates opportunities for others to succeed.

- **True success extends to purposeful giving.** Your generosity in knowledge or any other form of giving creates change, builds community, and ensures that your contribution raises others.

- **Wealth isn't just about money, but about legacy.** Teach the next generation how to preserve and grow what you've built. The mission isn't over until they're ready to lead the charge.

CONCLUSION
MOT DE LA FIN

I HOPE THE stories, lessons, and personal experiences in this book have sparked something in you. Something that makes you rethink how you handle your finances, your savings, spending habits, and most importantly, how you invest in your future. My goal in sharing my journey was to help you prepare for the financial battles that life will inevitably throw your way.

Consider this book as your tactical playbook, designed to guide you toward positive outcomes and lasting success. Growing up in an immigrant family, I learned early what it means to start from scratch. My parents moved to Canada when I was less than a year old, leaving behind everything they knew. They had no wealth, no connections, no safety net, just a determination to build a better life. It was like being dropped into unfamiliar territory with no intel, no map, no backup. But through hard work, discipline, and resilience, we laid the groundwork for a solid foundation. My parents always said, "If you want to live well, go to school and save your money." Sound familiar? For many of you, it might echo the advice you've heard countless times: Work hard, don't spend too much. Save more. And while that's solid advice, it's only half the mission.

In the military, you know that showing up, following orders, and performing well are critical, but that's only half the picture. Real success also requires strategy, adaptability, and foresight. The same applies to finances. Hard work alone won't secure your financial future; you need a plan, discipline, and the right gear in your arsenal. Let these insights guide you, so you can walk with confidence, purpose, and determination toward building the wealth you deserve. *Mission success starts here!*

Back to your duties. Dismissed!

ACKNOWLEDGMENTS

TO THE CAF, thank you for forging a life where purpose defines every chapter. Whether grinding through field exercises or navigating the chaos of deployment, this organization gave me a family and a calling. The grit I learned in the field, the trust built in the barracks, and the pride of wearing the uniform have shaped me. This book isn't just words—it's a nod to every leader and NCM who pushed me harder and every troop who reminded me why we serve. I salute the institution that made me who I am.

To the Chiefs, Warrants, and Officers who never settled for "good enough," your example stuck with me. You didn't just teach me to read a map—you showed me how to lead when the plan falls apart. From mentoring a fresh private to trusting me with a section, you proved that leadership isn't about rank, it's about raising others up. I'll always carry the lessons from those midnight debriefs and shared rucksack walk rants.

To the soldiers, lifelong learners, and friends who walked this path with me, thank you for your camaraderie, wisdom, and tireless encouragement. Your resilience, humour, and shared thirst for excellence propelled this project forward. Recognition goes to my inner circle—your patience in brainstorming, candid feedback, and faith turned an abstract vision into something tangible.

To my greatest ally and the most extraordinary woman I know, Christine. You've earned every one of those "Military Spouse" patches. You held down the fort during my time away, courses, exercises, and tours, and still had my back when I dived into this madness. Marrying a soldier isn't for the faint of heart, but you've turned every posting into an adventure. This book's my "thanks" for every unpacked box, every reintegration meltdown, and every time you reminded me why this life's worth fighting for. Love you to the FOB and back.

CHAPTER
CALLBACKS

Chapter 1 After Action Report

- **Financial literacy is mission-critical.** Just like tactical readiness, understanding budgeting, saving, and investing is essential for long-term success. Without financial literacy, even high earners can struggle to build wealth.

- **Your mindset is your strongest weapon.** Financial discipline, focus, and accountability are what separate thriving service members from those just getting by. Treat wealth building like PT—consistent, uncomfortable, but worth it.

- **Every CAF member has millionaire potential.** With the CAF pension as a solid base and smart, strategic planning layered on top, even average earners can retire comfortably and wealthily with the right habits.

- **Set financial goals using a military-grade strategy.** Define your financial mission, break it into OPERA-style goals (Organized, Practical, Effective, Results-driven, Accountable), and prioritize based on urgency and impact.

- **Start where you are—and start now.** Whether you're new to the CAF or halfway through your career, the most important step is beginning. Financial preparedness is non-negotiable, and the sooner you take action, the better your long-term outcome.

Chapter 2 After Action Report

- **Diversify your income sources to boost wealth building.** The Wheel of Wealth framework will enhance your cash flow by exploring various sources of income or upskilling opportunities to pursue higher-paying roles within the CAF or beyond.

- **Setting goals, saving money and tracking progress are key.** Define your specific financial objectives, save as much as possible, create a detailed budget, and invest those savings wisely. This approach is key to building and growing your wealth.

- **Create a financial safe bunker before it becomes critical.** Begin with a modest emergency fund and gradually expand it to cover a larger portion of expenses for an extended period. Automate your savings for effective results.

- **Spend purposefully to avoid negative progress.** Monitor every dollar, reduce discretionary spending, and avoid lifestyle inflation. Eliminate excess and prioritize what truly adds value, and remove financial distractions.

- **Engage debt aggressively before it compounds.** Focus on eliminating debt. List your debts, prioritize high-interest ones, and apply the snowball or avalanche method.

Chapter 3 After Action Report

- **Educating yourself on investment opportunities will help you make informed investing decisions.** Explore stocks for growth, bonds for stability, or real estate for long-term gains, each with a varying level of risk, return, and accessibility.

- **Understanding your financial limits is key to a solid foundation**. Choose an investment that matches your unique financial profile, whether you are cautious or aggressive. Carefully select assets that align with your time horizon and goals.

- **Stay attuned to market conditions for smarter moves**. Monitor trends, economic shifts, global events, and local changes that affect your investments. This will enable you to adapt your strategies proactively as needed.

Chapter 4 After Action Report

- **Start the right investment account to support effective growth**. Whether you choose TFSA, RRSP, FHSA, or a Non-registered Account, this fundamental step ensures your resources are allocated strategically, laying the foundation for effective wealth-building management.

- **Allocate your assets for maximum growth**. Strategically allocate your funds across various assets (stocks, bonds, ETFs, real estate, etc.), based on your goals, risk tolerance, and time horizon. This will ensure diversification and optimize growth.

- **Counteract market conditions effectively**. By setting a clear timeline with specific investment goals, whether short-term or long-term, keeping a timeline will guide your decisions, help you track progress, and allow for adjustments as market conditions evolve.

- **Conduct regular reviews for maximum performance**. Consistently evaluate your investments and overall portfolio performance. This will ensure you stay on course, adapt to market shifts, and adjust to optimize returns.

Chapter 5 After Action Report

- **Overcoming personal fear is crucial when making financial decisions.** As anxiety often originates from uncertainty, past mistakes, or lack of knowledge, it can paralyze you.

- **Emotional decision-making can derail financial progress.** Eliminating debt requires behavioural changes and strategies that reduce harmful spending and encourage healthier financial habits.

- **Hidden costs and expensive habits can consume your resources unnecessarily.** Redirect funds toward wealth building by identifying financial leaks that quietly drain your bank account. Cutting these non-essential expenses helps free up money for your financial goals.

- **Commitment to upskilling ensures long-term wealth accumulation.** Pursuing financial growth involves continuous learning, and seeking mentorship or resources enhances decision-making.

- **Avoiding common financial mistakes.** Focusing on trivial expenses that add no value distracts you from wealth-building priorities. Failing to build an effective entourage, delaying your investment journey, and gambling your money away limit growth opportunities.

Chapter 6 After Action Report

- **Financial stability post-service starts with clear retirement planning.** Identify your personal goals, align them with your pension and other sources of income, and apply proactive wealth management practices to ensure long-term financial security.

- **Understand available resources at retirement to counter unforeseen challenges.** Prepare for life's uncertainties with backup options, like your pension fund, RRSP, investments and social security benefits, to create a reliable buffer for navigating money crises effectively.

- **Ensure CAF retirement safety with preparedness**. Assess your retirement savings, including CAF pensions and RRSP contributions, to confirm preparedness. Regular contributions during service, combined with leveraging tax benefits, will help grow your retirement fund, securing financial stability for life after service.

Chapter 7 After Action Report

- **Choose the right financial team for success.** Pick advisers whose values and goals align with yours. Choose those who genuinely care about your future and have the expertise to guide you toward your financial objectives.

- **Build your financial entourage and optimize your support**. Seek out experienced individuals who have been where you want to go. Successful people leave a trail. Connect with them and learn from their journey.

- **Keep your comms clear at home for less vulnerability**. Financial silence within a family leads to confusion and leaves everyone exposed. Open conversations about money, goals, and planning turn your household into a mission-ready unit. The more your loved ones know, the better prepared they'll be for life's battle.

- **Share what you've learned to help others grow**. Teaching your family and peers about financial discipline is a legacy move. Share what you've learned, lead by example, and help others rise. That's how real leaders build strong communities, both in uniform and beyond.

- **Your money, your mission, your move**. Whether you use an adviser or go solo, take ownership. Keep learning, ask questions, and stay engaged. You're in command, making your financial choices with intention and confidence.

Chapter 8 After Action Report

- **Financial independence is the freedom to choose how you live and control your time.** It's built through education, disciplined saving, and smart, consistent investments. With a solid plan, you gain the freedom to choose your next mission on your own terms.

- **Mission review is critical to progress**. Assess your income, investments, and returns. What worked, what didn't, and why. If something underperformed, pivot and adapt. Rebalance your portfolio, diversify, and make sure your strategy still aligns with your goals.

- **True wealth carries responsibility**. Share your knowledge, mentor others, and lead by example. True leadership creates opportunities for others to succeed.

- **True success extends to purposeful giving**. Your generosity in knowledge or any other form of giving creates change, builds community, and ensures that your contribution raises others.

- **Wealth isn't just about money, but about legacy**. Teach the next generation how to preserve and grow what you've built. The mission isn't over until they're ready to lead the charge.

RESOURCES

Bank of Canada. 2025. Monetary Policy Report - January 2025. https://www.bankofcanada.ca/publications/mpr/mpr-2025-01-29/.

Bank of Montreal (BMO). Savings Calculator. https://www.bmo.com/main/personal/bank-accounts/savings-accounts/savings-calculator/.

Canada Revenue Agency. 2025. "Registered Retirement Savings Plan (RRSP)." Government of Canada. https://www.canada.ca/en/revenue-agency/services/tax/individuals/topics/rrsps-related-plans/registered-retirement-savings-plan-rrsp.html.

Coffeestics. Average Cost of a Cup of Coffee in Canada 2025. https://coffeestics.com/countries/canada.

Clason, George S. 1926. The Richest Man in Babylon. Penguin Books.

Finviz Sector Map 2025. https://finviz.com/map.ashx.

Housel, Morgan. 2020. The Psychology of Money: Timeless Lessons on Wealth, Greed, and Happiness. Harriman House.

Intuit Education. 2025. Intuit Education Home: https://education.intuit.com/home.

Kiyosaki, Robert T. 1997. Rich Dad Poor Dad: What the Rich Teach Their Kids About Money That the Poor and Middle Class Do Not!. San Mateo, CA: Plata Publishing.

MarketWatch. 2025. MarketWatch. https://www.marketwatch.com/.

Ontario Veterinary Medical Association (OVMA). 2025. Pet Care. https://www.ovma.org/petcare.

Ramsey, Dave. 2003. The Total Money Makeover: A Proven Plan for Financial Fitness. Thomas Nelson.

S&P Dow Jones Indices LLC. 2025. S&P 500 (SP500). Federal Reserve Bank of St. Louis. https://fred.stlouisfed.org/series/SP500.

Statistics Canada. 2024. "Household Saving Rate, 2021, 2022 and 2023." Government of Canada. https://www150.statcan.gc.ca/n1/daily-quotidien/241107/cg-a002-eng.htm.

Statistics Canada. 2025. Consumer Price Index. https://www.statcan.gc.ca/eng/dai/btd/cpi.

Tim Hortons. 2025. Coffee Menu. https://timhortonsbreakfastmenu.ca/coffee-menu/.

Yahoo Finance Canada. 2025. https://ca.finance.yahoo.com/.

ABOUT
THE AUTHOR

I WAS BORN on February 9, 1986 in a refugee camp in northern Thailand. That same year, my family and I made a bold journey across continents to start a new life in Canada. We were among the first Lao immigrant families to settle in the country. I grew up in the vibrant, multicultural city of Montreal, where French became my first language. It was there, while studying at Collège Rosemont and later taking university-level language courses at UQAM (Université de Québec à Montréal), that I developed a strong appreciation for communication and culture.

In 2005, driven by a deep sense of purpose, I joined the Canadian Armed Forces as an artillery gunner. After several years of service, I discovered a new path and transitioned to become a Meteorological Technician in 2012, later graduating from the CAF School of Meteorology in Winnipeg.

Since then, I've proudly served as a weather forecaster with the Royal Canadian Air Force, supporting missions both at home and around the globe. Throughout my career, I've witnessed the blistering deserts of Africa and the freezing landscapes of Alaska. These experiences have tested me, shaped me, and deepened my commitment to service. I've been honoured with recognition as a decorated soldier, but for me, it's always been about more than the uniform—it's about making a lasting impact for those who come after me.

I'm married to my wonderful wife, Christine, and together we share a love of travel and adventure. We're now preparing to grow our family in the coming years. With twenty years of service behind me, I'm also beginning to look ahead to retirement and a second career—possibly in finance, where forecasting markets might just echo the skills I've honed forecasting weather.

Outside of my military life, I have a quiet passion for old books, antiques, and music. I find peace in the smell of aged paper, the history in forgotten objects, and the keys of a piano. My journey has been one of duty, discovery, and dreams—and it's far from over.

www.buildingwealthwhileserving.com